# PRAISE FOR
## *SOLVING YOUR MONEY PROBLEMS*

"Almost everyone has money problems. Few have money solutions. David Crank's *Solving Your Money Problems* shows how faith principles can be your solution for a rich and prosperous life."

**Christopher Ruddy**
CEO, Newsmax Media, Inc.

"Pastor David Crank writes about fundamental biblical principles that should be applied to every believer's life. His financial story is inspiring and relevant; it is a great tool for anyone wanting to get out of debt, change their financial situation, or just become a better steward of their money. *Solving Your Money Problems* is a much-needed lesson on the abundance God has for his children."

**Bobby Schuller**
Pastor of Shepherd's Grove
Author of *Happiness According to Jesus*

"So much of the Bible addresses our relationship with money, and yet so many people still struggle to understand their role as stewards in God's economy. In *Solving Your Money Problems*, David Crank challenges and inspires us to explore the financial attitudes and false assumptions that often rob us of the peace that comes from fully trusting

God. David offers biblical wisdom, practical suggestions, and personal examples that will force you to rethink your relationship with money and refocus on God as the source of all your blessings."

**Chris Hodges**
Senior Pastor, Church of the Highlands
Author of *Fresh Air* and *The Daniel Dilemma*

"As one who grew up with a poverty mindset, David Crank has always inspired me to see God as an abundant provider. His new book, *Solving Your Money Problems*, is both practical and faith-building. If you have money problems, God's truth is the solution."

**Craig Groeschel**
Pastor of Life.Church
Author of *Divine Direction*

"With humor, candor, sincerity, and conciseness, my friend David Crank tackles an incredibly important topic for anyone who wants to reach their redemptive potential. *Solving Your Money Problems* challenges us all to embrace the bounty of God's goodness for the purpose of God's glory. When we embrace God's generosity to us, we are able to demonstrate that generosity to others."

**Dr. Dharius Daniels**
Author of *RePresent Jesus*
Senior Pastor, Kingdom Church

"One thing is for sure: If you're not solving money problems, you're creating them! Thank you, David Crank, for helping us move our lives forward towards God's best."

**Kevin Gerald**
Champions Centre

"The message of Pastor David Crank's book is powerful, yet simple. Without God in your life, lots of things seem impossible. With God, nothing is impossible. Always put God first. Always give control to God. I've led a charmed life. I've experienced many miracles. Now I understand why. Study *Solving Your Money Problems* and experience your own miracles."

**Wayne Allyn Root**
Former Polical Commentator
Author of *The Power of Relentless*

# SOLVING YOUR MONEY PROBLEMS

# SOLVING YOUR MONEY PROBLEMS

DAVID CRANK

Fedd Books
P.O. Box 341973
Austin, TX 78734
www.thefeddagency.com

Published in association with The Fedd Agency, Inc., a literary agency.

Scripture quotations marked (ESV) are from the ESV® Bible (The Holy Bible, English Standard Version®), copyright © 2001 by Crossway, a publishing ministry of Good News Publishers. Used by permission. All rights reserved.

Scripture quotations marked (NIV) are from the New International Version®, NIV®. Copyright © 1973, 1978, 1984, 2011 by Biblica, Inc.™ Used by permission of Zondervan. All rights reserved worldwide. www.zondervan.com The "NIV" and "New International Version" are trademarks registered in the United States Patent and Trademark Office by Biblica, Inc.™

Scripture quotations marked (NHEB) are from the New Heart English Bible. Public Domain.

Scripture quotations marked (WBT) are from Webster's Bible Translation. Public Domain.

Scripture quotations marked (KJ21) taken from the 21st Century King James Version®, copyright © 1994. Used by permission of Deuel Enterprises, Inc., Gary, SD 57237. All rights reserved.

Scripture quotations marked (BSB) are from The Holy Bible, Berean Study Bible, BSB Copyright ©2016 by Bible Hub. Used by Permission. All rights reserved worldwide.

Scripture quotations marked (NASB) are taken from the NEW AMERICAN STANDARD BIBLE®, Copyright © 1960,1962,1963,1968,1971,1972,1973,1975,1977,1995 by The Lockman Foundation. Used by permission.

Scripture quotations marked (NLT) are taken from the Holy Bible, New Living Translation, copyright © 1996, 2004, 2007 by Tyndale House Foundation. Used by permission of Tyndale House Publishers, Inc., Carol Stream, Illinois 60188. All rights reserved.

Scripture quotations marked (KJV) are from The Authorized (King James) Version. Rights in the Authorized Version in the United Kingdom are vested in the Crown. Reproduced by permission of the Crown's patentee, Cambridge University Press.

Scripture quotations marked (AKJV) are from the American King James Version. Public Domain.

This publication is designed to provide accurate and authoritative information with regard to the subject matter covered. It is sold with the understanding that the publisher or author is not engaged in rendering finacial, accounting, or other professional advice, If financial advice or other expert assitance is required, the services of a competent professional should be sought.

ISBN: 978-1-943217-53-3
eISBN: 978-1-943217-54-0

Printed in the United States of America

First Edition 15 14 13 10 09 / 10 9 8 7 6 5 4 3 2

*For my wife, Nicole.*

# CONTENTS

# INTRODUCTION

## MY LIFE IN A TRAVEL TRAILER

My dad was raised by my grandpa, who didn't have any money. They grew up in the ghetto. When my father grew up and became a police officer, he did better for a while, but he wanted to go in the ministry, so he sold everything and preached all over the country as an itinerate evangelist. That's why I grew up in a travel trailer.

Life on the road quickly drained my dad's bank account, and the people he preached to didn't have any money. Our Cheerios were just O's. Our bologna didn't have a first name. Anybody know what I'm talking about here? We were poor! So that tiny trailer was where I slept, ate meals, and went to school. Our whole life was running around the country. My dad had a good heart, but he didn't understand everything in his Bible. When you don't know the truth, the truth can't set you free.

Eventually, my dad started praying and reading his Bible, which is a great idea for a preacher! He found out that the Bible says, "Let them shout for joy and be glad, who favor my righteous cause; And let them say continually, 'Let the LORD be magnified, who has pleasure in the prosperity of His servant'" (Psalm 35:27 KJV). He started reading things like, "Blessed shall you be in the city, and blessed shall you be in the country" (Deuteronomy 28:3 NASB). He realized that "it is He who gives you power to get wealth" (Deuteronomy 8:18 ESV).

Did you know that two-thirds of the parables in the Bible deal with *money*? Some religious people say, "Oh, money is the root of all evil!" But the Bible actually says the *love* of money is the root of all evil because those who chase after it wander away from the faith and bring misery on themselves (1 Timothy 6:10). You can love money and not have any money at all. But by itself, money is not bad. In fact, it can be good. Money can buy blankets for the homeless. Money can rescue girls out of sex trafficking. Money can build churches around the world. Money can pay for television time to take the gospel around the world. Money is not good nor bad; it's neutral.

So my dad started trying to believe what he was reading. He understood that when you give, it will be given back to you, good measure, pressed down, shaken together, and running over (Luke 6:38). I'm talking about net-breaking, boat-sinking, supernatural opportunities.

At first, it didn't look like anything changed. My school desk still served as our dinner table and still folded down to become my bed at nighttime. We didn't have any money. Our family sometimes sat around the little table as my dad prayed over invisible food because we couldn't afford anything to eat. He would tell my brother and me, "Just chew, boys, chew."

I thought my dad was straight-up crazy. We were acting like we were chewing a bologna sandwich, and I'm thinking, "If we're pretending, why have bologna? Let's imagine steak!"

It often brought him to tears, but he built a foundation of faith for my family and me so that we could go on and make a greater impact in the world. Like Simon Peter, we would learn to obey the words of Christ and launch "into the deep water" (Luke 5:4 NASB). But first, we had to learn some things. We had to search the Scriptures for truth. Then we had to put them into practice so that they would become visible in our lives. That's what I want to share with you in this book. God's principles are profound, yet practical. And best of all, they work every time.

There is a form of political correctness in the church

that says preachers can't talk about money. It's part of the plan of the Enemy to keep the church broke and out of the financial system because he knows what we will do when we get ahold of resources. We're going to help somebody! God has me on an assignment to write the book that will help you discover and obtain your financial freedom. So many people just need a roadmap to help them get where they know they need to go because they don't know how to get there.

Clearly God takes pleasure in the prosperity of his people. One of the reasons he gets pleasure is because we are able to help more people discover who he is and what he has done for them. If we're broke or hamstrung by a bank, we can't self-fund his agenda. The banks have high-rise buildings with gorgeous marble floors because of the money they receive from people who just learn to live in the system and pay interest.

You are different. I know because you picked up this book. You're the person who's going to follow the bread-crumbs and discover where true financial peace and freedom lives.

Before this book ever became a reality, my dad was teaching me what his dad failed to teach him. His father suffered through the Great Depression, and it scarred him. My dad had to discover God's truth for himself and put it into practice. Because he did, he left me a great inheritance. And it wasn't just the fruit of his labor; it was the root of his wisdom.

The world's system is designed to train us to sit in school all day, take a short break for lunch, and only when the bell rings are we "free at last, free at last!" But there's something on the inside of you that desires complete freedom, and that only comes from flowing in the great wisdom God has placed in his Word. Your rich dad actually is God, and he has placed a Bible in your hand with loads of proverbs to teach you things like, "In all labor there is profit, but mere talk leads only to poverty" (Proverbs 14:23 NASB) and "By humility and the fear of the LORD are riches, and honor, and life" (Proverbs 22:4 KJV). Your biological father may never have taught you anything about finances or living debt-free, but your heavenly Father did. And he sent me into your life right now to help you discover the nuts and bolts necessary to make it happen.

# CHAPTER 1

BREAK THE POVERTY MINDSET

I grew up with a poverty mentality. When we went to the gas station, we never dreamed of filling up the tank. We just put a couple dollars' worth of gas in the car. Often times we would go to the grocery store and write a check we knew wouldn't clear until a few days later. We would be in the grocery line and have to put items back because it was over the limit we knew would arrive in a couple days. This is no way to live.

After my daddy went to be with the Lord, I still went to the sale rack to buy a shirt. I always bought stuff on sale. Now I'm not against discounts. Thank God for them! But when you grow up eating air bologna, it's easy to develop that kind of mindset. That's the way I was raised, so that's the way I thought.

One day when I went to the store to buy that half-off shirt, I heard something inside say, "Don't buy that shirt." I just knew for some reason that God didn't want me to do it. He said, "You need to break this mindset, and you need to buy a nice shirt." So I did.

Now don't get me wrong. God is not telling everyone to go out and buy whatever they want. He's not against sale items or thriftiness. He was just doing a specific work in me. He needed to expand my thinking. My mindset was too small for what he wanted to do with my life. My poverty mentality had become a blessing blocker, holding me back from fully trusting him.

One of the reasons I love Psalm 35:27 is because it says, "Let the LORD be magnified, who has pleasure in the prosperity of His servant" (NASB). We are the King's kids. We all have a desire on the inside to live like a king because our father is the King of Kings. There's nothing wrong with this when it is done in balance. Every king has the ability to provide from his rich treasures. We are supposed to be amply supplied so that we can go about the King's business. But like me at a young age, many people have not discovered their rights and privileges as a believer.

Our church was able to bless four widows with brand new Volkswagen Jettas. One woman's husband had been murdered. Another woman had her own children, his child (her step-child), and an adopted child who had been born with an addiction to crack cocaine. All of these widows were in very tough situations, so for our church to bless them in such a way made a huge impact.

We take very seriously the proverb that says, "He who has pity on the poor lends to the LORD; He will reward him" (Proverbs 19:17 NEHB). This isn't some magic formula to get what we want from God. We don't do anything that is not led by the Spirit. We don't give to get; we give to bless. But let me tell you, God has blessed us so much that giving away four new cars doesn't seem all that impressive. We are continually impressed by the generosity of our God and strive to emulate that as much as possible.

Once you realize you are a child of the King and He takes pleasure in the prosperity of his children, you can break out of your poverty mentality. We need to come to God like the Canaanite woman in Matthew 15. She asked for mercy from Jesus, and he said that what he had was for his children. But she had a tenacity that wouldn't quit. She basically said she'd eat the crumbs off of Jesus' table, which was all the provision she needed. Just a little to get her healing. Her absence of pride and refusal to give up got Jesus' attention, and he provided for her. She didn't want to fake it until she made it. She needed something and wasn't worried about what people thought about her.

A lot of people in her situation might have acted like they were healed even though they were sick. That person who drives a fancy car by going even deeper into debt is living a false prosperity. But God hates pride. Poverty is a curse, and it's not God's plan for his children. But we have to empty ourselves to let him fill us up, even if it means admitting that we have caused our problems by not handling money according to his Word. When we do that, we begin to unlock the richness of his treasures in ways we never imagined when striving to gain things on our own. God doesn't hate when we have things; he hates when things have us. Realize now that he has a system in place to bless you, but it's according to his ways, not yours. Again, I stress that poverty is not God's plan for you. His plan is to prosper you. You just need to learn how to put yourself in the right position to receive his blessings.

> **THAT PERSON WHO DRIVES A FANCY CAR BY GOING EVEN DEEPER INTO DEBT IS LIVING A FALSE PROSPERITY.**

## THE GOD OF PLENTY

There's an incredible story that anyone in the church has probably heard. Jesus was preaching to 5,000 people gathered in the countryside. That didn't even count the women and children. Jesus had all of them listening to him all day, so when evening came the disciples said, "This is a deserted place, and already the hour is late. Send them away, that they may go into the surrounding country and villages and buy themselves something to eat" (Mark 6:35-37 NHEB).

Jesus put the responsibility back on them, saying, "You give them something to eat."

They asked, "Shall we go and buy two hundred denarii worth of bread and give them something to eat?"

Right there, we know something many people overlook. How could they buy food for all of those people if the disciples didn't have money? What is sad to me is that followers of Jesus Christ oftentimes buy into the mindset that the church should be broke, which means we cannot help people. But that wasn't the case with the disciples. In the parable of the vineyard, each worker was paid a denarius for a day's work, so 200 denarii equaled about 200 days of pay. That's about ten months of your salary! There was no lack with Jesus' disciples, and there need not be lack with his followers today. Of course, on that day, Jesus had different plans.

Jesus tells them not to buy bread. One of the disciples probably admitted they didn't know where to go anyway. There's no Sam's Club in the area, no Costco. Where would they get enough bread? Then Jesus says something interesting. He says, "How many loaves do you have? Go and see."

The disciples looked around and gathered what food they had and reported back to Jesus, "Five loaves and two fish."

Obviously, that's not enough. But Jesus told them to bring what little they had and watch how God works. They bring it to Jesus, put it in his hands, and Jesus breaks it, blesses it, and lifts it up in prayer to God.

All of a sudden there was so much multiplication they began to share the food, and everyone ate. And it wasn't just a snack. The Bible says that everyone ate until they were satisfied. Nobody went hungry. They were full, and twelve baskets full of bread and fish were left over.

See, God is not a God of "just enough." He's the God of *more than enough*. He is not El Cheapo; he is El Shaddai. He is Jehovah Jireh, which means "the LORD will provide." He wants to meet all of your needs and the needs of other people. "The blessing of the LORD makes rich, and He adds no sorrow with it" (Proverbs 10:22 ESV). When God makes you rich you don't have the sorrow and all that interest money paid to the bank. There's no sweeter feeling in the world than to look at all your bills and see nothing owed. And there's nothing sweeter than driving a car knowing it is completely paid off. When you're out of debt you're not concerned about income because it takes very little for you to live.

Now they go back to the little lad, and they give him

these twelve baskets that are left over. This kid was living large in the Land of Plenty! I'm sure there were people saying, "What in the world is that kid going to do with all that? He doesn't deserve so much!"

I believe the boy got to walk away with all of the reward because he took a risk. He was the only investor. There is never any reward without risk, but there really is no risk when you are doing business with God. He repeatedly says he wants to bless you.

"Blessed shall you be when you come in, and blessed shall you be when you go out" (Deuteronomy 28:6 ESV). He will "command the blessing on you in your storehouses, and in all that you set your hand to; and he shall bless you in the land which the LORD your God gives you" (Deuteronomy 28:8 AKJV). But you've got to give it to God. Like that boy, you have to say, "God here's what I have. I give it to you." Everyone in his family got to partake of the rich resources God bountifully blessed him with because he was obedient to put Jesus first.

Now here's the big kicker. God will ask you, at some point in your life, to give him everything. People say, "Someday when I get blessed, then I will bless God." Not true. We never get around to it.

We must say, "God, here I am. Use me and send me." But know that when you do fully trust him, it's never for less. It's always for more. He will continue to multiply your resources when you obey him. Get this truth in your heart and mind: he is the God of plenty.

## FROM THE PIT TO THE PALACE

Jacob, father of the Israelites, returned to his promised land of Canaan with his eleven sons, the youngest of whom was Joseph. Soon after returning, Benjamin was born, which made twelve sons and, eventually, the twelve tribes of Israel. But his favorite was Joseph.

Maybe you've heard of that musical *Joseph and the Amazing Technicolor Dreamcoat*. That's based on Joseph in the Bible. His father gave him "a tunic of many colors" (Genesis 37:3), which was so cool it made his older brothers jealous. They hated him. To make things worse, he had dreams—big dreams. Now Joseph was about seventeen years old, and you know how teenage boys are. They're not too smart. So Joseph told his brothers about his dreams. In them, all his brothers bowed down to him.

Can you imagine that? This punk teenager telling his ten older brothers they were going to bow down to him? But that's what he did. If you think they hated him for the coat, you know they must have really hated him for these dreams. Joseph told his father, Jacob, and even Jacob rebuked him, saying, "What is this dream that you have dreamed? Shall your mother and I and your brothers indeed come to bow ourselves down to the earth before you?" (Genesis 37:10 ESV).

Then the passage says, "And his brothers envied him, but his father kept the matter in mind" (Genesis 37:11).

See, his father was smart. He knew that sometimes you've got to listen to these things. Sure, Joseph might be a teenage dreamer, but he might be hearing from God. So Jacob kept an open mind.

Back in those days, Jacob's boys were shepherds. Ten boys with ten families means a lot of sheep, so they would walk for miles. They'd stay out for weeks or months at a time. So the ten older brothers are out with the sheep, and Joseph and his kid brother, Benjamin, are at home. Jacob starts wondering if all his sons are alright. Or maybe he's worried about his sheep, I don't know—it doesn't say. Anyway, he sends Joseph out for like fifty miles on foot. Joseph walks for days only to discover they've gone another fifteen miles away to a place called Dothan (not the one in Alabama!).

So he keeps walking. How many of you know that sometimes you just have to keep walking? You've got a mission in life, and just when you think you should be there, somebody moves the goalposts. Sometimes the best thing to do is just put one foot in front of the other and keep going.

Anyway, Joseph finally finds his brothers out in the hills of Canaan. He sees them from a long way off, and they see him, too. You know how they knew it was him? The Bible tells us that they said to each other, "Here comes the dreamer!" (Genesis 37:19 NIV) They literally called him a dreamer (in their language, of course). And they didn't mean it as a compliment.

Has anyone ever called you a dreamer, and not in a good way? Let me tell you today that if your dream is from God, it's a great thing to be a dreamer. Hold on to those dreams and declare that they will come to pass. Just be aware that some people will hate you for it, like Joseph's brothers. Before the teenager had even gotten to where his brothers were grazing their flocks, they plotted against him. "Let's throw him in a pit and tell Dad he was eaten by a wild animal," they said. Then they mocked his visions from God, saying, "We shall see what will become of his dreams!" (Genesis 37:20 KJV).

One brother, Reuben, didn't want Joseph killed, so he came up with an idea. "Shed no blood, but cast him into this pit which is in the wilderness, and do not lay a hand on him" (Genesis 37:22 KJV) He thought he could come back later and let Joseph out, so he did.

There are many ways you can find yourself in a pit. Sometimes your enemies put you there. Maybe, like Rueben, someone thought they were actually doing you a favor by putting you in a pit. I'll even go out on a limb and say that some of you have dug your own pit and jumped in all by yourself! If you dug your own pit of debt, ask yourself this question: Why would God continue to reward bad behavior so that you increase your debt and make yourself a slave? He wants us to live in freedom. He said that the Son has set us free indeed. Oftentimes pride and ego are the biggest deterrents to reducing expenses. I have found that you can shop at discount stores and look just as cool as someone shopping at the expensive ones. It's all in the way you wear it!

Regardless of how you got there, a pit in the wilderness is a bad place to be. But that's where Joseph found himself. After God gave him dreams and his father treated him with favor, his own brethren threw him in a pit. Even worse, while he was down there with no food or water, the Bible says they then sat down to eat a meal. Can you imagine that? You're stripped of your cool coat, thrown in a pit by your family, and they chill out to a nice dinner! And just when he thought things couldn't get worse, they did.

Some Ishmaelites (descendants of another ungodly plan gone awry) pass by, and a few of the brothers pull Joseph out and sell him as a slave. Before Reuben even knew what was going on, his evil brothers were profiting from their deceit, and Joseph goes from being the favorite son to an Egyptian slave. He's gone for good. His brothers even dip his coat in blood to fake his death for their dad.

Now let me ask you this: Do you think maybe Joseph's

faith in God was shaken at this point? Do you think he was tempted to forget his dreams and accept his lot in life as a slave in a foreign country? If there was ever a circumstance for someone to think that God wanted him or her to settle for less than his best, this was it. But that's not what Joseph did. While we don't know everything he went through, we know that he was sold to a powerful man in Egypt named Potiphar. Potiphar was Captain of the Guard under Pharaoh, so he had a nice house and beautiful wife. Even though Joseph was his slave, we are told "that the LORD was with [Joseph] and that the LORD caused all that he did to succeed in his hand" (Genesis 39:21 ESV)

Do you see that? Even in slavery, God prospered Joseph! His brothers put him in a pit and made him a slave, but God made him prosper, even in a place that wasn't his home, surrounded by people who weren't of God. Have you been mistreated? Are you surrounded by godless people? God has not forgotten you! He still has a plan for you, and the dreams he gave you are still valid. He will prosper you wherever you are. But don't get comfortable yet. The Enemy will continue to throw you temptations and trials. Such was the case with Joseph.

As I mentioned, Potiphar had a beautiful wife. Joseph, a young single man living in her household, probably saw her every day. He wasn't blind, and he certainly wasn't dead, so he probably noticed how good-looking she was.

Then one day while his master was out of the house, she comes to him and says, "Lie with me." That's a nice, biblical way of saying, "Let's get it on!"

Being a man of God, Joseph refused. But she didn't give up. Over and over, she kept coming to him, trying to get him into bed with her. Now I don't care how great a man of God you are, that's just not fair! To be young and single, living in a nice house with a beautiful woman coming on to you all the time is more than most men can handle. But Joseph was strong. He had been to the "True Love Waits" purity conference. He was waiting on jmatch. com to find that perfect Jewish girl.

Then one day, Potiphar's wife grabs him, and he tries to get away. They wrestle a bit, and she pulls off his tunic, which is an outer garment. Joseph runs away, basically in his underwear, and she's furious. All her efforts to take advantage of him have failed, so she screams for the household guard, and they come running. "He came in to me to lie with me, and I cried out with a loud voice. And it happened, when he heard that I lifted my voice and cried out, that he left his garment with me, and fled and went outside" (Genesis 39:14-15 ESV).

Later, when her husband came home, she told him the same thing, showing him Joseph's tunic as proof. Let me tell you, there's no trouble like the kind of trouble a guy finds himself in when he is caught messing with another man's wife! And though Joseph was innocent, who was Potiphar going to believe—a Hebrew slave or his own wife? So in one day, this man of God goes from being an honored servant in a powerful household to being an inmate in the king's prison.

Still, Joseph never forgot the Lord's call on his life. He didn't give up on his God-given dreams. And God never gave up on him. True to his nature, the Lord "gave him favor in the sight of the keeper of the prison" (Genesis 39:21 ESV).

Do you understand the pattern here? Let me spell it out for you. God gives Joseph a dream. His enemies try to take it away by putting him in a pit or a prison. Joseph remains faithful to God, and the favor of the Lord follows. God prospers him. At the end of the chapter that lands Joseph in prison, it repeats the same thing that it said when Joseph was sold into slavery in the first place: "the LORD was with him; and caused everything he did to succeed" (Genesis 39:23 NLT).

How many of us could prosper in prison? That may seem illogical. To the world, it is. But God doesn't look at our earthly condition to determine our heavenly position. The fleshly eye would look at Joseph and see a pathetic prisoner under the thumb of the king of the land. But the spiritual eye sees a prosperous potentate under the hand of the King of the universe.

Joseph didn't whine or complain in prison, even though he was there for two years! How many of us would think God had forsaken us after two *days*? But Joseph felt God's favor, even in prison. He went about the business of God's kingdom as if he had never been displaced, disrupted, or discouraged. He had a dream from God and never doubted whether or not it would come true.

In what I think was a bit of a confirmation of his dreams, Joseph eventually got out of prison by interpreting the dreams of others—first a fellow prisoner who was restored to his position serving Pharaoh, then to Pharaoh himself. In the king's dreams, he saw seven years of abundance in the land, followed by seven years of famine. Of course, the king didn't know it when he had the dreams, which was why Joseph had to interpret them, but once he realized it, the king appointed Joseph to oversee the storage process.

So during the seven years of abundance, Joseph made sure food was harvested, stored, and kept secure for the coming famine. That means he had officers under his command. Get that—he was a former slave and prisoner now commanding Egyptian officers! Skeptics probably hated him, but he had Pharaoh's authority over him, so they kept quiet. I would imagine he also had to build tons of barns or grain silos or whatever they built in Egypt to preserve food. (I'm pretty sure they hadn't invented freeze-dried packaging yet.) He was in charge of the entire affair, sort of Governor of Famine for the whole country, so I'm sure everybody knew who he was.

Oh yeah, he also got a new ring, a nice new suit, a gold necklace, a fancy chariot, bodyguards, and a hot wife. (Okay, it just says the daughter of a priest, but if the jewelry, clothes, and ride all looked good, why not the wife?) See, when God prospers you, he can do it any way he wants. Sometimes he may want to use you in that difficult place, but I don't believe he wants you to stay there forever. And even while you're there, he wants to prosper you in all you do.

Joseph had to go through the pit to get to the palace. Then he had to go through prison to get to the position where his childhood dreams would come true. When the abundance turned to famine and the surrounding lands faced starvation, only one place remained the Land of Plenty, and it wasn't Canaan. It was Egypt. Eventually, Jacob sent his other sons to Egypt to buy some bread, where they unknowingly stood in front of Joseph. Then they bowed. Just like in the dreams.

What does this teach us about having a poverty mentality? It demonstrates how our focus leads directly to our results. Joseph never focused on the betrayal and all the bad things that happened to him. He looked beyond the pit and the prison. He experienced pressure from all directions but kept his eyes in one direction and followed the dream God gave to him. Stay faithful to the Lord and focus on his plans, and you will prosper in all you do.

## MAKE ROOM FOR THE SUPERNATURAL

According to Siri, that magical voice on my iPhone, the word "supernatural" refers to "a manifestation or event attributed to some force beyond scientific understanding or the laws of nature." When God takes hold of your life, including your finances, things will happen that nobody can explain. God wants to put his "super" on your "natural," but the answer is not chapter 11 bankruptcy. The answer is chapter 23 truth: "The LORD is my Shepherd. I shall not want" (Psalm 23:1 KJV)

We tend to get comfortable with the things that are regularly available to us. From groceries and a roof over our heads to family members who are around us, this becomes our comfort zone. In Joshua 5, the Israelites were comfortable with God's supernatural provision of manna on a daily basis. But then the manna stopped. Why? It wasn't because God wasn't interested in providing for them. It wasn't because he quit doing supernatural things. It was because he wanted to move them to the next level.

When the people first saw the manna, they probably thought, "What is that?" As they grew accustomed to eating it, though, manna became the norm. When it stopped, they wondered, "Where is it?"

This happens to all of us. God provides that job, and soon we depend on the job more than the God who provided it. We depend on the supply and forget about the Supplier. That's usually when God decides to switch things up. He wants to move us out of our comfort zone and on to the next level. He also wants to remind us that he always provides when we trust and obey. We have to learn to walk in faith. He will give us a vision, and then he will give us provision for the vision.

> MY DAD TALKED ABOUT THE LAND OF LACK, THE LAND OF EVEN, AND THE LAND OF PROSPERITY— WHAT I LIKE TO CALL THE LAND OF PLENTY.

My dad talked about the Land of Lack, the Land of Even, and the Land of Prosperity—what I like to call the Land of Plenty. Too many Christians live in the Land of Lack, feeling like there's more month than there is money. They want to give more, but don't have more to give. Nobody argues that the Land of Even is an admirable place to be, where you owe no man anything except love. But I don't believe we are just supposed to survive; I think we are supposed to thrive. I'm telling you that God wants to lead you to the Land of Plenty, not for your glory, but for his.

Psalm 112 describes a blessed person. It says, "Blessed is the man who fears the LORD, who delights greatly in his commandments. His descendants will be mighty on earth; the generation of the upright will be blessed. Wealth and riches will be in his house, and his righteousness endures forever" (Psalm 112:1-3 NASB).

Does God want you to be blessed? Yes. Does God want you to fear him and delight in his instructions? Yes. Does he want to bless your family? Yes. And does he want to put wealth and riches in your house? Yes! Wealth isn't the goal; it's a byproduct of living in obedience to God. If your finances are jacked up, you need to ask Jesus right in the middle of your mess, and he will turn the mess into a message.

Walt Disney was a crazy guy with a dream based on a mouse. The same mouse he talked to as a kid to get through hard times became his great provider. People made offers to buy his dream, but the dream was so real that he couldn't sell the mouse. It seems a little crazy to build your dreams around a mouse, but sometimes it takes a little crazy to do something special.

In our cold trailer in the winter, I would often get the flu. I remember playing video games as a kid, and as I raced through each level of the game I'd envision myself being a champion for other people by helping them through their challenges. I wanted to reach people and help them, but I knew I couldn't do it sick and broken. It was a little crazy, but it was a dream God gave me. I just had to overcome that poverty mindset so I could actually fulfill my dream.

Everyone has a dream planted inside of them. But unless a grain of wheat falls into the ground and dies, it remains alone; but if it dies, it produces much grain (John 12:24). The prodigal son went to the pigpen before the feast at his father's house. Daniel went to the lion's den before the throne of power. Joseph went to the pit before the palace. David had spears thrown at him and was chased into the wilderness by King Saul before he ever became king. Between the promise and the provision, there's always a problem. Don't get bogged down in the problem because that's not your destiny. Keep your eyes fixed on the promise and provision because that's where God wants you.

Do you want to give up? Do you feel stuck in the Land of Lack or content in the Land of Even? Don't let someone else live your dream. Get up one more time and say, "I have a dream!" God is compelling *you* to live your dream, not somebody else. In order to do that, you need to make room for his supernatural work in your life today and every day. God has a purpose for you. You are called, you have favor, you are anointed, and God is compelling you in your heart to live your dream.

Psalm 24 says, "The earth is the LORD'S, and all its fullness, the world and those who dwell therein." Do you realize that all the wealth of the world comes from the earth? Obviously crops like coffee and wheat come from the earth. Gold and silver are mined from deep within the ground. But even things like microchips are made from sand, and plastic comes from crude oil and natural gas. There is nothing that doesn't come from the earth, and God owns it all.

King David wrote, "The LORD will give what is good; and our land will yield its increase" (Psalm 85:12 ESV). Jesus himself said, "What man is there among you who, when his son asks for bread, will give him a stone? Or if he asks for a fish, will he give him a serpent? If you then, being evil, know how to give good gifts to your children, how much more will your Father who is in heaven give good things to those who ask him!" (Matthew 7:7-11 NASB). It makes no sense to think that God wants us to live in the Land of Lack when it's clear that he is the owner of all wealth and wants to give his children increase and good gifts.

Financial need, pressure, and worry can choke the Word of God in your heart. They are frustrations and distractions that can prevent you from getting on with the dream he put before you. I know because I've been there! I have lost sleep worrying about finances. I've seen the economy tank and wondered, *God, are we going to make it here?* The Lord gave me this "wow" moment. He said, "Until you control your mind, you can't control your money."

Do you get that? God wants us to think on his terms, not according to the latest news. He wants us to buy into his system, not settle for the world's. He wants us to believe that he will meet all of our needs according to his riches in glory (Philippians 4:19). We need to be reassured that he will not forsake the righteous, which means those bought and paid for by the blood of Christ, and that his kids don't ever have to beg for bread (Psalm 37:25, Romans 3:22). We have to throw out those negative thoughts that go against God's promises. God has a purpose for you and your money—and it's to not go broke! You are to build God's kingdom and leave an inheritance for generations. What you do should impact others for Christ long after you're in heaven. That's the plan.

The Enemy wants you to break down before you break through because he knows it will impact your children and your children's children. It's far more than just leaving financial wealth to your grandkids. It's the legacy of knowing how to get money, keep money, and use money for his kingdom, instead of being used and abused by the world's financial system. Prosperity is God's idea, but you have to live according to his words in order to achieve it. Worldly prosperity is not the same. When you die, you can't take it with you. But godly prosperity leaves its mark for generations. If you've been handling your finances in the natural, doing things your way instead of God's way, then you need to step aside and make room for his supernatural guidance. The way to do this is not to focus on money or getting rich; it's by focusing on him, believing and practicing his Word, and pursuing his kingdom above all else.

Like Joseph, you may be in a prison of your own right now. But God has a bigger plan for you. Don't forget the dream he has given you, and don't let anyone take it from you. Even Jacob kept his son's dream "in mind," leaving a sliver of hope for God to do something great. It's time to acknowledge the fact that the Land of Plenty was designed by God for his people, and he's ready to put you there. My dad taught me at a young age to never discount God's supernatural ability to cancel debt. I can't begin to tell you how many people have come up to me after a service and told me an incredible story of debt cancellation. It is true that if you take one step toward God, he will take ten toward you. I'm about to walk you through several steps on the path to the Land of Plenty. As you take these steps, you

> DON'T FORGET THE DREAM HE HAS GIVEN YOU, AND DON'T LET ANYONE TAKE IT FROM YOU.

will see God walking with you.

# CHAPTER 2

## REELING IN THE DEBT

The United States was born in debt. The country that revolted against England's "taxation without representation" soon found itself forced to implement tariffs and taxes to deal with the fledgling nation's debt. Despite some efforts to reduce it, things like wars, recessions, and expanding government programs kept driving it up. At the end of World War I, the national debt hit $25 billion. Near the end of the Great Depression in 1939, it was over $40 billion. After World War II, it soared to $241 billion. By 1995, it was up to $3.6 trillion—that's 3.6 million million![1] In 2009, it was at $10.6 trillion. By the end of 2016, it doubled.[2] That's compound interest at work. Suffice it to say, the federal government has set a good example of a bad practice by spending way beyond its means, and most

Americans do the same thing.

At the end of 2015, 38 percent of all households carried some sort of credit card debt. The average American had an unpaid balance of $5,700. And the total outstanding U.S. consumer debt was a staggering $3.4 trillion![3] America is a nation enslaved to debt.

In today's world, it's too easy to spend money we don't have to impress people we don't like with things we don't need. I like to call one of the more well-known debt traps "Max That Card." As you probably know, when you spend more money than you have, there's going to be distress and discontent. You're not going to enjoy your life.

Proverbs 22:7 says, "The rich rules over the poor, and the borrower is the servant to the lender" (NASB). In other words, credit card companies are keeping you on a short leash through high interest rates. Have you ever looked at your bill and thought, "I can't possibly owe $3000!" And then, on further investigation, you realized you were spending five or ten dollars at a time. What happens is we do it without thinking.

There's an acronym for DEBT: Doing Everything But Thinking. I'm here to challenge you to think about your money: where it's going, what it is or isn't doing, and why you should take control of it by giving up your control and allowing God's principles to dictate how you manage it.

Financial experts will tell you to lay out a budget and

stick to it. Write down everything you're spending and take a hard look at it. Don't take an easy glance at it. This is not easy. Our sinful nature wants to take the easy way out, but sometimes we need to take a hard look at things and head down that difficult road of change. I guarantee that most of us are buying things we don't need and paying prices we don't need to pay. The first step to getting out of debt is to THINK about everything you buy.

> GOD SUPERNATURALLY HELPS YOU GET OUT OF DEBT. PSALM 37:4 SAYS, "DELIGHT YOURSELF IN THE LORD, AND HE SHALL GIVE YOU THE DESIRES OF YOUR HEART."

I want to go on record and tell you I'm not against having nice things. You should have nice things. God wants you to drive the best, live in the best. But when you try to add blessing to yourself, you can get in debt and be discontented. When you do it God's way, God supernaturally helps you get out of debt. Psalm 37:4 says, "Delight yourself in the LORD, and He shall give you the desires of your heart" (NASB). He'll give it to you. You don't have to add it to yourself. And when the desires of your heart line up with him, you'll find you need a lot less than you may think.

Debt is a monster. The bigger it gets, the more it towers over you like a giant.

It reminds me of an old parable about a farmer who owned an old mule. The mule fell into the farmer's well. The farmer heard the mule braying, or whatever mules do when they fall into wells. After carefully assessing the situation, the farmer sympathized with the mule, but decided that neither the mule nor the well was worth the trouble of saving. Instead, he called his neighbors together and told them what had happened . . . and enlisted them to help haul dirt to bury the old mule in the well and put him out of his misery.

Initially, the old mule was hysterical! But as the farmer and his neighbors continued shoveling, and the dirt hit his back, a thought struck him. It suddenly dawned on him that every time a shovel load of dirt landed on his back, he should shake it off and step up! This he did, blow after blow. "Shake it off and step up . . . shake it off and step up . . . shake it off and step up!" He repeated this over and over again to encourage himself. No matter how painful the blows or how distressing the situation seemed, the old mule fought panic and just kept right on shaking it off and stepping up!

It wasn't long before the old mule, battered and exhausted, stepped triumphantly over the wall of that well! What was meant to bury him actually blessed him, all because of the manner in which he handled his adversity.

If we face our problems, respond to them positively, and refuse to give in to panic, bitterness, or self-pity, the adversities that come along to bury us usually have within them the potential to benefit and bless us.

But like a boy in the Bible, when you have God on your side, you can slay that giant. Everyone in the Valley of Elah had the ability to march forward and slay Goliath, but only one man had the necessary discipline and tenacity to make it happen. When David came at Goliath, he came at him with his mouth open. Your victory in the valley won't happen until you move—often when your mouth moves! The Bible says you don't have some things because you haven't asked for them (James 4:2). So you need to open your mouth and ask God for them. This is not about short-term gratification so you can feel good about your finances. It's about long-term purpose so you can do all that God leads you to do. Life is a marathon, not a sprint.

We eat good by the fruit of our mouths (Proverbs 13:2). Often when you're having a negative thought or being tempted by materialism, you can open your mouth and address it. You're at the mall, and you think you need those shoes or those clothes or that brand new smart phone. Those things are screaming, "Buy me!" Now, don't start screaming back at things in the mall. That will just get you kicked out. But you can interrupt that voice with your own voice.

There is something in the power of speaking out loud. "Let the weak *say* 'I am strong'" illustrates the power of positive confession. It's not denying reality when we deny our weak nature and choose God's strength. For example, you would be right in reminding yourself verbally:

- I do not need to buy what I cannot afford.
- I'm taking massive action to win a massive victory.
- I'm choosing long-term purpose over short-term pleasure.
- I'm doing what God wants me to do so I can do more of what he wants me to do.
- I will not allow the Enemy to eat the fruit of my labor.
- I am choosing God's blessings not just for myself, but for generations to come.
- I am grabbing on to riches and honor in one hand and length of days in the other.
- I look to God for peace and prosperity, health and wellness, wisdom, and direction.

These types of confessions, when based on God's Word, serve to center us on his will. They recalibrate our minds, focus our intentions, and galvanize us for his plan for our future. So when temptation comes, and the lust of the flesh tries to steer you off course, open your mouth with the Word of God and submit to his will, not yours.

Sometimes you have to say *no* to now so you can say *yes* to later. Psychologists call this "deferred gratification" and tie it to success in life. The more you can focus on the greater rewards to come, the more you can resist settling for less.

John wrote, "Beloved, I pray that you may prosper in all things and be in health, just as your soul prospers" (3 John 1:2 NHEB). There's a prosperity that has to first happen in your mind. Then it happens in your body. I believe it should happen in your wallet as well.

## A GODLY INHERITANCE

When my dad decided to live debt-free, things got radical in our household. We lived in this beautiful little house in St. Louis. I came home one afternoon, and my dad had the front door wide open. People were coming in and out of our house like crazy. He decided to have an estate sale without telling any of us. He was literally selling the pictures off our wall! He sold everything. At the end of the day, the house was vacant, but he had loads of dough.

We said, "What are you doing?" He said, "You know, I was reading about debt reduction and how to do it. I'm not going to get an extra job, but I'm going to reduce our debt."

As a result, his credit score was really good. He beat bankers at their own game. He paid that house off in a record amount of time. Not long after that, we moved to another house, and he paid it off in twenty-two months. How'd he do it? Through a big salary? No. Through self-discipline and denial. Through contentment.

Scripture says that "godliness with contentment is great gain" (1 Timothy 6:6 NIV). Contentment basically says that you might not *have* the best of everything, but you can *make* the best of everything. My dad went really radical on this one. He was modeling discipline. He said, "I'm going to sell my motorcycle." We said, "Wow, Dad, we can't believe you'd give that up!" And then he printed out the amortization schedule on the house and marked off the payments he could make with the proceeds from the motorcycle and said, "Look how many years ahead we will get."

He did this consistently. He printed out his schedule and hung it on the wall where he could see it every day. He set a vision in front of us all. He used a blue pen to mark off his regular payments. Then he used a red pen to mark off additional principal payments. When you look at the sample amortization schedule, you'll notice that the principal payments are relatively low early on. So each time my dad would pay one or two or three additional principal payments, he'd have this big chunk of red marked off. Then he'd add up all the money he would save by knocking out the interest payments and got real excited—so excited, he actually wrote a song.

*We're out of debt*
*Our needs are met*
*Got plenty more*
*To put up in store*

He'd go around singing that crazy song, celebrating his path to financial freedom. It was all because he went through the simple step of printing out his amortization schedule and then took the more difficult steps of practicing discipline to wipe away the debt.

Let me show you how this works. An amortization schedule is how much of your house payment goes toward the actual loan and how much goes toward interest, which is the bank's profit. Just take a look at this actual schedule for a thirty-year loan of $200,000 at 5 percent interest:

| PAYMENT | AMOUNT | INTEREST | PRINCIPAL | BALANCE | INTEREST PAID |
|---|---|---|---|---|---|
| Month 1, Year 1 | $1,073.64 | $833.33 | $240.31 | $199,759.69 | $833.33 |
| Month 2, Year 1 | $1,073.64 | $832.33 | $241.31 | $199,518.38 | $1,665.67 |
| Month 3, Year 1 | $1,073.64 | $831.33 | $242.32 | $199,276.06 | $2,496.99 |
| Month 1, Year 2 | $1,073.64 | $821.04 | $252.60 | $196,796.66 | $10,754.03 |
| Month 1, Year 3 | $1,073.64 | $808.11 | $265.53 | $193,682.05 | $20,523.13 |
| Month 1, Year 5 | $1,073.64 | $780.25 | $293.39 | $186,966.60 | $39,575.12 |
| Month 1, Year 10 | $1,073.64 | $697.11 | $376.53 | $166,930.94 | $83,958.06 |
| Month 1, Year 20 | $1,073.64 | $453.50 | $620.15 | $108,219.08 | $154,083.38 |
| Month 1, Year 30 | $1,073.64 | $93.85 | $979.79 | $21,545.33 | $185,510.39 |
| Month 12, Year 30 | $1,073.64 | $4.45 | $1,069.19 | $0.00 | $186,511.57 |

So your monthly payment here is $1,073 and change. The first month, you're paying $833.33 to the bank in interest and $240.31 toward the loan. Do you get that? You're paying over a thousand bucks, but less than 25 percent of that is actually going toward your debt. This goes on for over three years! Imagine how far ahead you would get if you just paid an extra principal payment of $250 a month for those three years. (Some financial experts advocate things like paying on your house every two weeks instead of once a month or doubling your principal payments each month. All these things are great because they cut way down on the interest and significantly reduce the length of your loan.)

Look a little further down. You can see that your principal-to-interest ratio finally flips so that you're paying off your debt more than you're handing money straight to the bank. It's actually in the sixteenth year, which means that for more than half of the time you're paying off your house, you're paying the bank more than you're paying off your debt. When you finally make your last payment on that $200,000 loan, you will have paid the bank $186,511. That's money you will never see again. In fact, to pay off your $200,000, you shell out $386,511. That's crazy!

These numbers probably aren't your numbers, but the point is the same. Find out what yours are. Ask the bank. They have to tell you. Putting the actual numbers in front of you will help set a vision and give you the power to make smart decisions.

Now our house wasn't worth $200,000 back then, but the interest rates also weren't at 5 percent. In fact, average rates back then were two and three times that, so the interest amounts were obscene. That's what my dad was looking at, and that's why he went fanatical on us. He had a vision of building a church, but he didn't have the money. When he looked at his amortization schedule, he saw the money! Simply by paying off the principal payments, he could stop giving money to the bank and put himself in a position to build a church. Before he achieved financial freedom, he received perceptual freedom. He could see a way to fulfill his dream.

So many people are in a prison of debt, but it begins as a prison of the mind. God wants you to be debt-free, but do you? Once that becomes the desire of your heart—a true and powerful longing—then God will begin to work to give it to you. Why? Because it's his desire for you. But in order to obtain such a massive result, it requires massive action.

That's what happened with my dad. He started making massive changes. He even sold his beautiful Cadillac. I mean, he had this gorgeous, two-tone model with a moon roof. I'm like, "You're selling that? That's your car, man!" My dad was cool, like Magnum P.I. cool, if you remember that TV show. Dad had the mustache and hair like Magnum. The car was part of the way he rolled. But he sold it.

Then he bought a 1979 Pinto. The primary colors were primer and bondo. In the evenings, he would get my brother and me out in the garage, and we would fix that car up. He would open the hood, and we would power wash it. He'd spray paint underneath it. We beat out the dents and painted it. It wasn't the fanciest car, but it allowed him to do radical debt-elimination, and it freed him. And by taking great care of the car and improving it through hard work, he actually increased its value.

My dad could have worked an exorbitant amount of hours so he could afford a nice car. But instead he said, "I'm not going somewhere in a fancy car and not see you kids. Y'all are going to be with me." He taught me that you can be a dollar ahead or a dollar behind. He left me a godly inheritance.

If you remember, the Bible said that God wants us to leave an inheritance to our children's children. That is not just the inheritance of dough, money, fruit. No, he wants us to leave the root. If you can leave your kids the root, they can continue to produce the fruit. People often say, "I want to raise good kids." I don't. I want to raise good adults who become big time—and ones who get out of here so I can live in my house alone! People raise good kids, and then their kids are forty and still want you to pay their bills. Don't do that. Raise good adults. Inheritance. It's not about the fruit; it's about the root. The root keeps producing through diligence. The root keeps producing by putting God first. The root keeps producing by just being smart.

When you try to add it to yourself through debt, you're not up any more; you're down, just like everybody else. You end up having problems. You may end up having to work several jobs, which usually creates family problems. But if you'll reel in the debt, reel in the lust, and don't budge from the budget, you can get out of debt.

## BETTER THAN GOLD

I know a lady who was a massive producer of income. She retired with enough money to last a lifetime. At least, you would think it was enough to last that long. The problem was that she knew how to make money, but she didn't know much about managing money. Pretty soon, she was living that proverb that says, "For riches certainly make themselves wings; they fly away as an eagle toward heaven" (Proverbs 23:5 KJV).

Here's another proverb that talks about wisdom: "Length of days is in her right hand, and in her left hand riches and honor" (Proverbs 3:16 KJV). This woman I know had half of that wisdom. She gained "riches and honor," but she couldn't make them last for her "length of days."

Her one-handed approach led her to blow through her retirement way too fast. Her rock-star attitude toward spending money left her broke at an old age, which forced her to go back to work. We have to get both hands on our finances by practicing godly wisdom in managing our finances.

The Bible says, "How much better to get wisdom than gold! To get understanding is to be chosen rather than silver" (Proverbs 16:16 ESV). With all your getting of money, don't forget the more valuable thing: wisdom. What is wisdom? It's the ability to understand the information in God's Word and apply it to your life. It's living by godly principles. Proverbs says of wisdom, "her proceeds are better than the profits of silver, and her gain than fine gold" and "she is more precious than rubies" and "in her left hand [are] riches and honor" (Proverbs 3:14-16 NKJV).

We all know how valuable precious metals are. I have a friend who bought gold when it was around $350 an ounce and sold it when it hit $1900 an ounce and paid off his house! Silver and gold are good (not the paper certificates, but the real thing), but God has something even better.

If you're struggling with debt, which is a lack of money, God offers you something more valuable than gold. You're probably focused on rubies, silver, and gold, in a sense, when what you really need is true wisdom. Chasing a paycheck brings misery. Peace and joy are fruit of the

Spirit, but worrying about that pile of bills robs you of both. The solution is not to go after more money, but to get a giant, godly dose of wisdom. Once you have wisdom, you'll be in a far better position to obtain wealth, and you'll know how to handle it.

"The one who gets wisdom loves life; the one who cherishes understanding will soon prosper" (Proverbs 19:8). You may be struggling now, but if you seek wisdom and understanding, there's a promise coming soon.

You may be wondering, *How do I get wisdom?* I've got good news: God is waiting for you to ask. "If any of you lacks wisdom, let him ask of God, who gives to all liberally and without reproach, and it will be given to him" (James 1:5 NHEB). That word "liberally" has nothing to do with politics. It means "freely" and "generously." God wants to pour out his wisdom in your life, starting today. And he does it "without reproach," which means there is no expression of disapproval or disappointment. He won't shame you for admitting that you have made a mess of things. Just the opposite is true: he will rejoice when you finally confess your shortcomings so that he can come in and fill the gap. He can't wait for you to ask because he is more than ready to give you what you need.

The foundation is already laid out for you in his Word: "For the LORD gives wisdom; from his mouth come knowledge and understanding" (Proverbs 2:6 NIV). Putting that into action requires you to know his Word and hear his Spirit. By studying the Scriptures and knowing his voice, you can live a Spirit-led life and walk out of the Land of Lack straight into the Land of Plenty. The path is called wisdom.

A pastor I know took out one loan after another until he had gotten himself and the church completely upside down. He had sold his house, his cars, and even his and his wife's wedding rings just to make a few more payments. When people in his church found out, many lost respect for their leader, expecting him to be wise and diligent. People left the church, and the financial problems spiraled out of control.

I think, deep down, every pastor has a strong desire to reach more people. Carrying out this desire requires wisdom, not just for pastors, but for everyone. Dumb decisions can backfire on us. When the bank starts taking all of our money, and we can't spend more to help people, it's like dying a little every day.

Matthew 5:8 says, "Blessed are the pure in heart, for they shall see God" (ESV). If you want to see God work in your life and ministry, make sure your top priority is people helping hurting people. People are moved to invest in a church organization when they see lives being changed. They can only get so excited about a great building. Saving souls must be the primary goal.

Back to my dad's story: We were out in a field mowing when he felt prompted to drive about five miles to fill the tractor with diesel fuel. He thought, *Why would I do that? I'll just fill it up with the gas can.* Had he driven the truck and used the gas cans, it would have taken less time, but he would have missed his moment. Timing's everything. So he drove the tractor to the gas station.

As he arrived, he noticed there was a 1960 Corvette following him. He got off the tractor at the gas station and noticed the driver of the Corvette was carrying the title. The guy asked my dad, "You wouldn't know anybody who wants to buy this car today, would ya? I lost my job, and I have to sell this car right now. I'm taking it to the wholesalers, but I hate to sell it to those crooks."

My dad said, "Absolutely!"

See, my dad had given up his '60 Corvette when he went into the ministry. He tithed it into what God had called him to do, positioning himself for blessing. Years later, he had learned how to get out of debt, bless others, and always put God first. By the time that old Corvette showed up behind him at the gas station, he had $3,500 in the bank, which is what the guy needed. Over the years, things like that happened eight more times, so when my daddy died he had eight of those sports cars in his garage. He was a collector. And that first $3,500 car ended up selling for a huge profit. I sold them all because I didn't need those cars. But I learned the value of investing and saving. If my dad didn't have the $3,500 in the bank, he would not have been in a position to act when the opportunity presented itself. He demonstrated how to get out of debt, build God's kingdom, create strength through savings, and invest as the Spirit led.

My dad was also living out that promise Jesus made when he said there is "no one who has left home or brothers or sisters or mother or father or children or fields for me and the gospel, who shall not receive a hundredfold now in this time . . . and in the age to come, eternal life" (Mark 10:29-30 NIV). Notice how Jesus distinguished between "in this time" and "the age to come." A poverty mentality gives up everything now and expects nothing in this life, but Jesus said it's coming "in this time," and it's coming back a hundred times! When my dad obediently sold his car to go into the ministry, God knew good and well that he was going to bring that car back to him and bless him with several more.

What my daddy left me was far more valuable than a few cars because he didn't just leave the "fruit" of his wisdom; he also left the "root" of understanding. That's what God wants for you and your children. He wants to get you out of debt, take you to the next level, and bless you for generations.

## PRACTICAL STEPS

When you get out of debt, it's the sweetest feeling in the world. It frees you. It's liberating. You can help people. You can bless people. You can even bless your kids. What I don't want to do, though, is allow the legacy that my dad started with me to stop with my kids. I'm teaching my kids to teach their kids.

Here's a simple plan to start moving from the Land of Lack to the Land of Even, and eventually, to the Land of Plenty. That's your God-given destination, so it's time to start moving there with confidence.

**List all debt.** The first step to reeling in debt is to list everything you owe. Big or small, write it down or put it in a spreadsheet—however you manage things best. When you look at your overall debt, the devil will whisper in your ear, "You'll never do it." Know right now that is a lie from the Father of Lies. If you need to write some Scriptures on your list, do it. I've given you plenty already, and there's more to come.

Don't focus on the grand total. List them out line-by-line so you can look at them individually. Alone, they are not so scary. That's where you start. Each one is a marker on your path to victory.

**Set goals.** It's important for you and your family to set goals so you all know what you are working toward. I recommend paying off small accounts first. Get rid of that $200 debt and have a victory lap. Then pay off $500. Oh yeah! You don't get in debt overnight, and you're not going to get out overnight, but if you don't grow weary in well-doing, you will reap. Instead of your pocketbook being marked by defeats, you will start living victory to victory. When unexpected setbacks pop up (and they will), just add it to your list of goals. Don't let that hurdle become a wall. Make it another cause for celebration when you get over it.

Sometimes you need to reward good behavior with a future incentive. Put on your refrigerator, "We're going to Tahiti when it's done." Or "Here's what we're going to buy when it's done." My dad illustrated this when he paid off our house in twenty-two months. As promised, he bought me a go-cart. Not just any go-cart, but the ultimate go-cart with a van body. It was unreal. He said, "That's the fanciest one, right?" I said, "Yeah." And that's the one he bought. I was the only little player in a van body driving down the street in our neighborhood because he made good on his promise.

**Work hard.** Proverbs 10:4 says, "Lazy hands make for poverty, but diligent hands bring wealth" (NIV). That means the way out of poverty is to not have a "slack hand." What's that? It's the attitude that says, "It's too hard. Nobody else does it. I don't want to get up early. I don't want to work late."

Diligent work is a necessary component of prosperity. Yes, that can mean hard work, but it also can mean smart work. Wisdom teaches you how to maximize your efforts for the greatest gain. It's like my dad refusing to skip out on his family in order to pay the bills and instead choosing radical debt reduction. He worked hard, but he also worked smart. This comes into play when dealing with your existing debt.

If God leads, and you have peace about it, work overtime, or maybe take an extra job for a season. Be intentional about it. If it means sacrificing time with your family, lay it out for them. Set a goal of paying off debt, stick to your budget, put that extra-job money straight toward the debt, plan an exit strategy to end that job, and celebrate with your family when it's paid off.

**Live below your means.** Before I was a pastor, Nicole and I were able to retire in our early thirties. She worked very hard in her corporation. She's a very smart businesswoman, making a ridiculous commission some months. I loved it. We would go places, and people would ask me, "What do you do?" I'd joke, "I'm a go-getter. I take her to work, and then I go-get-her." But even with the success, we still shopped at thrift shops. We didn't subscribe to all the premium channels on cable. We still were frugal.

Today, we're still blessed. I still buy pants on sale for

$10. I'm not saying you can't buy fancy things. I am free from a poverty mentality, but that doesn't mean I'm wasteful. I am saying you can't buy things you can't afford with money you don't have. That has to stop now.

Another thing you can do is not go to an overpriced coffee shop. Stop paying $5 for a cup of coffee when you can make it at home. It's just coffee! The same is true for restaurants. A few years ago, I got in the habit of driving through a burger joint every morning because my son liked their burgers. He would get two of them for five bucks and eat them on the way to school. Nicole found out, and she's like, "You're spending $5 a day on burgers? That's $25 a week!" I'm thinking, "Yeah, so what?" Then she did the math and said, "$25 a week is $1,300 a year!" That got my attention. Then she said, "And he doesn't need to be eating all that junk anyway." Of course I couldn't argue with that, but the thing that stuck out to me was how a little a day adds up to a lot.

Most people with debt don't even realize how much money they are wasting by eating out. My advice is this: learn to cook! Today we have a lot more resources than when my dad was doing this. We have the library of Google. We have the University of YouTube. You can learn most anything online, from tying a bow tie to building a bomb (please don't do that). Certainly you can learn to make a latte or cappuccino. Use the internet to find easy-to-make, healthy meals that cost a fraction of the over-sized portions and junk food you're getting at restaurants. I'm not saying you should never eat out. I'm just saying that if you need to reel in some debt, cooking is usually one of the easiest ways to do it. (And if you do eat out, use a coupon!)

You might want to have a yard sale to get rid of stuff you don't use. Or maybe do it the twenty-first century way and sell it on eBay or Craig's List. Sometimes we need to eliminate the things we don't use when they drain us financially. A few years ago, God used the story of the maidservant and Elisha (2 Kings 4:1-7) to urge me to sell one of my "man toys"—you know, those expensive items that guys buy and then leave sitting around gathering dust? In the story, a servant girl had lost her husband, and her debt piled up so high that her creditors were going to take her sons as slaves. Thankfully, we don't have that today, or a lot of kids would be in literal bondage!

So Elisha says to her, "What do you expect me to do? Can't you sell something in your house?"

She says, "I don't have anything . . . well, except for a jar of oil."

He says, "Go borrow a bunch of empty vessels from your neighbors, then go in your house with your sons and shut the door behind you."

That part about shutting the door is what God stressed

to me. Sometimes you just need to shut the door on the things you don't use. Get rid of them. Sell them and use the money for something better. It will eliminate clutter around your house, and you can turn that free space into debt reduction.

With the maidservant, Elisha instructed her to pour out her oil into the empty vessels, which she and her sons did. They had so much oil that they sold enough to pay her debt and still had some left over to use for themselves. Sometimes we don't realize that we already possess the means we need if we will just obey God.

I would also encourage you to negotiate the debt you do have. "Ahhh, it's easier to just pay the bill," you might say. But I'm telling you, no. *Negotiate*. Don't get lazy when it comes to credit cards. Call your current credit card provider and tell them, "I'm thinking about moving my business to another credit card because they're offering me a better rate." See what they will offer. The worst they can do is leave you in the situation you're already in. It's a little work, but it will almost always save you money.

There are more ways than I can list to reduce your expenses, and everyone's situation is somewhat unique. This is where you need to be led by the Holy Spirit. God really doesn't mind if you pray and ask him to show you where you can cut back or reduce waste. The old adage that says, "it's the little foxes that spoil the vine" is true.

It tends to be many small things that bring us ruin, so it requires diligence and know-how to trim in all the right areas. God is eager to give you the wisdom that will show you the best ways for you to live below your means so that you can have more for him and his purposes.

**Stay disciplined**. Want to double your money? I'm going to tell you how. Fold it up and put it back in your pocket! *The quickest way to get out of debt is to add no new debt.* Make your flesh submit to God by saying, "I'm going to put the credit card in a block of ice in the freezer so it has to thaw out before I can use it." Think before you swipe! Maybe even go in for plastic surgery and cut it up. Get rid of it for a while. Self-discipline is a fruit of the Spirit-led life, so put it into practice with your finances. Stick to your plan, reduce your debt and expenses, and prepare to step into a your new life of plenty.

Don't tempt yourself. Stay out of the mall if everything you walk by yells, "Buy me!" You may think you need it, but you're gonna get home and a week later think, *Why did I buy that?* You really don't need everything your greedy little eyes see!

When I was a kid, I took really good care of my first bike. I polished the spokes on the wheels so they wouldn't rust. I think one of the keys to prosperity is appreciating what you have. Otherwise, you'll always want something more, which always drives you into debt. When people add stuff to themselves by just swiping a credit card, they don't even take care of the stuff very well because they don't dream about it, work for it, or save until they can actually afford it. That's why paying cash can force you to really think about what you're buying and bring you more in line with the will of God. I can't tell you how many times Nicole and I decided to pay cash for something, and by the time we saved up enough cash, we both said, "That's a dumb thing to buy. We don't really want that!" So going slowly and waiting on the Lord to add things to us keeps us from making foolish and impulsive decisions. Let's face it: you and I can both walk through our homes and point out things we'd take back if we could. If someone offered you cash for everything you don't want or need, you'd probably end up with a pile of money!

Learn how to be content. Luke 6:38 says, "Give, and it will be given to you." When you're in the cycle of debt your entire life you're like, "I can't afford to give." Why? "Because we're giving 18 percent to this credit card. We're giving 12 percent to another card. We're giving 8 percent to the car. We're giving 5 percent to the house." There's no percentage left for God. And there's no percentage left for you.

You need to be able to give to the church. You need to be able to give to others in need. And you need to be able to take your family on some kind of trip and enjoy it.

I believe God is tired of his children living in the Land of Lack. He wants to bless us, but can he trust us? Sometimes we don't need more money. We need more information and revelation to give us wisdom and power.

Part of that wisdom is found in Paul's ability to be content in any situation. Being content doesn't mean settling for less than God's best. It means being at peace regardless of the circumstances around you because your joy isn't found in your situation, but in your salvation. When you abide in Christ, and he abides in you, as he instructs in John 15:7, you can ask what you want, and it will be done. You will find that Christ is enough—always and forever. He may give you stuff to help you further his kingdom, but you won't feel the need for more stuff. You can tell you're in the right place when your desire is not for more stuff, but for more of him. You will be both content in him and also able to receive more.

**If you use credit, don't let it abuse you.** Some people advise to only pay cash. Generally, buying on a cash basis gives God a stronger voice in what you do. Many church projects have been done by the will of man and not the will of God. People just run right out and get a loan, and the bank typically doesn't take the Holy Spirit into consideration. If you have a good credit rating, lenders only have interest in your interest—as in money.

When we pray, seek God, and save up for a project,

many times we have less of our flesh involved when it's time to pull the trigger. Sometimes when you look at a pile of cash that you've saved, you suddenly have clarity of vision and realize you can use that money for something more urgent or beneficial, like paying off debt. When we listen to God instead of obligating ourselves to a loan, we are less likely to make wrong decisions and more likely to be increased supernaturally. If God leads, he provides. But many times we ask the bank to provide money that we're actually using for our *own* ideas and vision. I know there have been times in my life when I have gotten ahead of God. He has given me a desire to do something, but I did the deal on my own timeline with borrowed money, so I did not fully benefit from the investment. Paying with cash can slow you down, hone your focus, and help you avoid mistakes.

Of course, if you have cash, you don't need credit. But if you need credit, learn how to make the system work for you so that you don't work for the system. Get a word from God on it. Seek him for the wisdom and a specific plan. My dad had the "credit chat" with me when I was fifteen years old. He had me get a secured credit card where I had to put $300 on the card, and then I couldn't go over that limit. I bought and purchased items and then immediately wrote checks to pay the card. I was never surprised by a large credit card bill at the end of the month because

I paid it off all throughout the month.

A young man who worked for me found a great deal on a home that was repossessed by a bank. He had no debt because he didn't use credit cards or any other form of credit at all. He was tired of paying rent on a house and wanted to invest in a home instead. I told him that I'd help him with the down payment by giving him a bonus of several thousand dollars.

He was excited and set to go. But he couldn't get a loan. Why not? It wasn't because he had bad credit. It wasn't because he didn't have the down payment. It was because he had *no* credit. It sounds crazy, and in many ways it is, but because he had never used or abused credit, the system was now abusing him. He missed out on a house that went way up in value and was stuck paying rent while he built his credit.

My dad used to tell my brothers and me, "Good credit is one of the most important things you can have. Someday, you're going to want to buy something, and you will only be able to do it if you have good credit." So pay your bills, not just on time, but early. Don't let the system use or abuse you; learn how to use it.

By the way, please avoid what I call "fancy financing." I won't mention any names, but I've known pastors who have gone so far out on a financial limb that the bank would only set them up on a "high risk" loan, which means that the first ten years or so are nothing but interest payments. So if, for example, a church bought a million-dollar property, they'd pay ten years on that property and still own a million dollars in principal. That's insane!

That's just one example of the many "creative" loans some lenders are doing. Here's what God has taught us in the past: If the banks aren't willing to do a normal loan, you probably shouldn't do it. If they don't believe in your ability to pay it off without any tricks or extra protection for themselves, that's a bright red flag waving in the breeze. Take it to the Lord and ask for his wisdom so you don't overextend or allow someone to take advantage of you. In Jesus' parable of the "unjust steward," he makes this observation: "For the sons of this world are more shrewd in their generation than the sons of light" (Luke 16:8 ESV). Oftentimes, this is still the case today. The world is smarter about worldly finances than Christians are. I'm saying that while you shouldn't trust the world's system to provide for you—only God can really do that—you *should* be shrewd when it comes to dealing with it. Use it, but don't abuse it. And never, ever let it abuse you.

Obviously, the easiest way to avoid being used and abused is to pay cash. The older I get, the more I become convinced that this is the best way to go.

**Invest in yourself.** I have a friend in Lakeland, Florida, who during the most successful years of his life lived off 50 percent of his income and used the other 50 percent to radically destroy debt. When the great crash of 2008 hit, he was in a unique position because he was free from debt. He told me that regardless of what happened in the economy, his future was bright. This is God's will. It's what living in the Land of Plenty looks like.

I have seen him make some very strong financial moves for himself and his family because of his decision to stay debt-free. He still thinks radically when it comes to managing money. He saves money by eating at home. He spends very little for entertainment because he built a home theater with cash, so those expensive nights out for dinner and a movie don't exist for him. They enjoy home-cooked meals and watch movies or sports in the safety and comfort of their own house. People love to visit because he's got it all right there, and it costs him hardly anything. He invested in himself instead of turning that money over to others.

I want to point out the difference between gardening and farming. Some of you may have a few tomato plants or fruit trees in your backyard where you grow and consume. That's great. But that's not the same as forty acres of corn or wheat that a farmer might have. When that farmer sows into his field, he's not just taking care of himself and his family; he's sowing for greater wealth. Saving and investing is a lot like that. Consider the 10-10-80 principle: yes, you sow into God's kingdom, but you also sow into your own wealth by saving. Then, when the Spirit leads, you can invest, create more wealth, and use it to further his kingdom.

That 10 percent you save will position you for a blessing that is coming your way. (It will also prepare you for an emergency that might otherwise plunge you into debt.) Investing in yourself is not bad; it's good! It just needs to be balanced with tithing and subject to God's direction.

**Hear and obey.** These are the first steps to victory. Once your mindset is lined up with the Holy Spirit, your debt will no longer control you because you will begin controlling it. You may have a mountain of debt today, but you can say to that debt, "Be removed and be cast into the sea" (Mark 11:23 KJ21). Don't doubt in your heart, but believe that those things will be done. You will get out of debt! In fact, the more you speak it out loud, the more it activates the supernatural power of God and keeps you focused. Your desire follows your attention, so if your attention is on buying something, that's all you'll think about. But if you focus on getting out of debt and pay attention to everything you spend, your desire to be debt-free will take control and keep you on track.

God told his people through the prophet Isaiah, "If you are willing and obedient, you shall eat the good of the land" (Isaiah 1:19). This is a big deal: you have to be willing to hear God *and* be obedient to his Word. When God says to tithe, you have to tithe. When he says to set up a budget, you have to set up a budget. When you hear him and obey, then you "eat the good of the land." That means you prosper. And when you're financially free, good deals move across your path, and you're able to move on those good deals. Because you are willing and obedient today, you reap the rewards tomorrow. With time, perseverance, and wisdom, you will get in the place God made you to be.

Here's a simple chart to help you begin framing a budget. First, write down your total normal income from all sources. Then take 80 percent of that (total income multiplied by .8). This is your target for your living expenses. Then allow 10 percent for tithing and 10 percent for savings.

|  | Monthly | Annual |
|---|---|---|
| Total Income |  |  |
| Living Expenses (80% ) |  |  |
| Tithing (10%) |  |  |
| Savings (10%) |  |  |

Now write down all of your normal expenses. This may take a while. Don't forget anything! Only by taking a hard look at your expenses will you gain an honest assessment of your financial situation.

| | Monthly | Annual |
|---|---|---|
| Mortgage/Rent | | |
| Property Taxes | | |
| Home insurance | | |
| Electricity | | |
| Gas | | |
| Water | | |
| Trash/City Services | | |
| TV and Internet | | |
| Phone (cell and/or landline) | | |
| Homeowners Dues | | |
| Yard/Pool Maintenance | | |
| Auto Payment(s) | | |
| Auto Insurance and Taxes | | |
| Gas | | |
| Auto Maintenance | | |
| Medical Insurance | | |
| Medical Expenses | | |
| Dental Expenses | | |
| Groceries | | |
| Dining Out | | |
| Health Club Dues | | |
| Entertainment | | |
| Vacations | | |
| Tuition | | |
| Other School Expenses | | |
| Clothing | | |
| Gifts (not tithing) | | |
| Lessons, subscriptions, etc. | | |
| Other (list all below) | | |
| | | |
| | | |
| | | |
| | | |
| | | |
| **Total Expenses** | | |

Now look at your total monthly and annual expenses. Compare that to the number next to "living expenses" in the first chart. You should have a pretty good idea whether or not you are handling your finances properly. If your total expenses dwarf your living expenses, you need some massive change. If it's close, then you're in for an easy fix. And if your total expenses are actually less than your living expenses, then congratulations!

You're probably reading this book because your actual expenses are greater than your budgeted living expenses. Take a few minutes to run through your itemized list and circle the ones that can change. Pray about each one— even your income. If you'll take this exercise seriously, you will be on the path to the Land of Plenty.

# CHAPTER 3

## CRACK THE CODE

**D**uring one of my sermons, I randomly picked somebody out of the congregation. I handed her my bicycle
lock and gave her the numbers to unlock it. She tried,
but couldn't do it. She was intelligent, and she had the
right numbers, but she failed. Why? Because I gave her
the numbers but did not give her the sequence. She had
things out of order. I knew the sequence, so it unlocked
immediately. So many times we don't put God first, and
we fail. Why? It's not because we don't know the right
things; it's because we have them out of order.

There's a story in the Old Testament that I love. Before
David became a great king, he had some hard times. After
killing Goliath, King Saul became jealous, and David fled
for his life. He ended up hiding in what was called the

cave of Adullam. The Bible says, "When his brothers and all his father's household heard of it, they went down there to him. Everyone who was in distress, and everyone who was in debt, and everyone who was discontented gathered to him; and he became captain over them. Now there were about four hundred men with him" (1 Samuel 22:1-2 NASB).

This is exactly where I found myself when Nicole and I took over the church many years ago. Pretty much everyone around me was "in distress" and "in debt." (Have you noticed how the two go hand in hand?) Don't get me wrong. There were some great people around, but the church had been broke and run-down for so long they were used it.

So my wife and I started cleaning up the finances and helping people change their minds about debt, money, and godly prosperity. I noticed that as we talked about money it didn't just get into people's personal or business practices, but it also touched painful areas, especially in marriages. And no wonder, because debt is a stressful situation that destroys peace, provokes couples to blame each other, and causes strife. Paul said that "a servant of the LORD must not be quarrelsome" (2 Timothy 2:24 BSB), so when financial problems come up, they need to be dealt with in the right way.

We started teaching basic principles of good stewardship, and it turned a bunch of people in debt into mighty warriors. So many individuals and couples got out of the cave of debt and became fruitful, prosperous, generous, and more effective for the kingdom of God.

If you feel like you're hiding out in a cave of debt and distress, you need to learn the code to crack open the blessings of heaven. It's not some cosmic secret; it's laid out in the Word of God. So pay attention, and like so many in my church, you can become fruitful, content, and prosperous.

## CAN'T TOUCH THIS

Do you ever wonder why God put that one tree in the middle of the Garden of Eden and said, "Don't touch this. It belongs to me"? It would have been so much easier to leave that tree out. But if God had done that, mankind would not have had a choice. And that's really what God wants—for us to *choose* him. He demands to be first, so the sequence is clear, but he leaves it up to us to decide.

> And the LORD God took the man, and put him into the garden of Eden to dress it and to keep it. And the LORD God commanded the man, saying, "Of every tree of the garden thou mayest freely eat: But of the tree of the knowledge of good and evil, thou shalt not eat of it: for in the day

that thou eatest thereof thou shalt surely
die." (Genesis 2:15-17 KJV)

From the very beginning, God gave us abundance.
Adam and Eve had the whole world. They lacked for
nothing. But God gave them a choice by saying, "Here's
the whole world, except for this one thing. I'm reserving
this for myself. Don't touch it!"

We know what happened. They took what was God's
and created a mess for themselves and everyone else. Still,
God made ways for people to approach him. One of these
ways was by bringing him an offering. In the story of the
two brothers, Abel brought the firstborn of his flock. This
was the fattest, best-looking sheep he had. He left the runt
of the litter back in the field; he didn't try to pawn it off
on God. But Cain brought "fruit of the ground" (Genesis
4:2-5 KJV) for his offering. People say his offering was re-
jected because it was not a blood sacrifice or because his
heart wasn't right or because they weren't the choice picks.
It kind of sounds like maybe he just picked up some rotten
fruit off the ground. Whatever the reason, God's like, "No
way." Cain got no respect, and it made him mad. God's
like, "Hey, Cain, what's the problem? You knew I had to be
first, but you haphazardly came up and said, 'Okay, God,
I have this big ol' offering for you,' but I can't accept it because it's not in the right order. Therefore, I can't unlock

your blessing because the sequence is wrong! I can bless your brother, Abel, because he put me first."

I hear people all the time say, "Man, I gave this big offering for God." But do you tithe, or do you pay all the bills first? The principle of the tree in the Garden of Eden is the same as the tithe. God says, "You can have all this, more than you need, but the first 10 percent is mine. I own that. It's set aside. Don't touch it."

There's this guy in the Bible named Abraham. God promised him that he would be the "father of many nations" (Genesis 17:5 KJV). But it takes God too long in Abraham's opinion. He's like, "Hurry up, God, my biological clock is ticking, and you are running out of time. Bring my breakthrough!"

Abraham kept trying to fulfill God's promise in his own way. He and his wife think, "If God's going to do something, he'd better hurry." They're getting too old to have children, so Sarah says, "You know what? We have that gorgeous twenty-something maid. Why don't you go to her, Abraham? I'm sure she could have a baby."

He's like, "No, I'm not supposed to touch her." But she said, "Just go to her. It's okay with me." And he's like, "Alright, if you want me to, I will."

So Abraham and this servant girl named Hagar produce this joker named Ishmael, who was not blessed by God. That just brings all kinds of problems, which always happens when we try to do things our way instead of God's way. God must be the center of it all. He's Lord *of all* or not Lord *at all*.

Then, miraculously, God blesses Abraham and Sarah with a legitimate son, Isaac. He is the promised child, the center of attention. But when he's about thirteen, God says to Abraham, "I think you love Isaac more than me, so I need to test you to bless you. I need you to take your firstborn son on a three-day trip. Take him up the mountain to the altar and sacrifice him."

Abraham must have looked like the little dude from that old TV show *Different Strokes*. "What you talkin' about, Willis? You want me to give you *my firstborn son?*"

"Yeah, he's the tithe."

"Really?"

So now, anxiety attack on day one, followed by anxiety attack on day two. It's a long walk with this young teenage boy. Then, they get there. Abraham straps Isaac down. He gets ready to sacrifice him. He's going to give God his first 10 percent. And then, right when he's getting ready to kill him, God sings, "STOP! . . . in the *naaaame* of love, before you *breaaaak* my heart." (That's not exactly how it's written, but I can imagine it's pretty accurate!)

The Bible says an angel told Abraham, "Do not lay your hand on the boy or do anything to him, for now I know that you fear God, seeing you have not withheld your son, your only son, from me" (Genesis 22:12 ESV).

See that? God says these cool words: *now I know.*

If Abraham had kept his son, he wouldn't have had more. If he had withheld the first from God, he would not have unlocked a huge blessing. But because he obeyed, God spared Isaac, provided a replacement offering, and made this promise to Abraham through the angel:

> By myself I have sworn, says the LORD, because you have done this thing, and have not withheld your son, your only son—blessing I will bless you, and multiplying I will multiply your descendants as the stars of the heaven and as the sand which is on the seashore; and your descendants shall possess the gate of their enemies. In your seed all the nations of the earth shall be blessed, because you have obeyed my voice. (Genesis 22:15-18 NASB)

God will test you to bless you. He also invites you to test him. He's not trying to take something from us; he's trying to give something to us. We're afraid that he will demand a sacrifice, but what he really wants is obedience. This is what he revealed through the prophet Samuel when he spoke to King Saul: "Has the LORD as great delight in burnt offerings and sacrifices, as in obeying the voice of the LORD? Behold, to obey is better than sacrifice" (1 Samuel 15:22 ESV).

We can be so set in our ways, and greed can take hold of us to the point where we can't really trust God. We try to figure it out our own way. We try to make our own Ishmael when we just need to say, "I am a legitimate child of God, and I choose to obey." We need the wisdom to know what God entrusts to us and what needs to be left alone. Then we need to obey his voice so we can get things in the right order so that he will unlock the blessings he has in store for us.

## THE FIRST FRUITS

These early Bible stories of Cain and Abel as well as Abraham and Isaac illustrate the order God has set up. He is first and nothing else. God revealed this code in the Old Testament and echoed it again through Jesus Christ in the New Testament: "You shall have no other gods before me" (Exodus 20:3 NIV) and "Seek first the kingdom of God and His righteousness, and all these things shall be added to you" (Matthew 6:33 ESV). Every time God spoke, he's like, "I'm first, not you or your family or your job or your hobbies. Me."

The problem is that people are naturally consumers. We consume, and consume, and consume. We eat it all.

Then we go to church like Cain and say, "Hey, God, I'm here to offer this to you right now." And God's like, "No you didn't. Really? I get the last?"

It's like when my wife and I go out on a date and I have my iPhone. She hates that. She'll say, "Please leave the phone at home," but I'm like, "No, I need this, I really need this." So she'll be talking to me over dinner, and I'm like, "Yeah, I hear you" as I'm on my phone. Then she asks, "What did I just say?" If I don't know, she takes offense. She says, "I need to be first. I need you to pay attention to me." When we get home after the date, I'm like, "I wish I had paid attention." You know what I mean! She's like, "You want a date—ask Siri!"

God deserves to be first. He gives us the sequence. He said, "I was able to bless Abel. I unlocked the blessing for him. I would not do it for Cain because he wouldn't get the sequence right."

It's not the tithe if it's not the first 10 percent. He said "prove me now here" in Malachi. Right after he says that we rob him by withholding the tithe, God explains what happens when we bring the first 10 percent to him. He says to test him on this. We can test God! He says if we'll do it his way, he will "open for you the windows of heaven and pour out for you a blessing until it overflows" (Malachi 3:10 NASB).

When God blesses you, you will know you have been

blessed. Your hard work won't go to waste. What you do will prosper. You won't have enough room for it all. And everyone will notice. But you have to get the sequence right. This is God's order of things, and he's waiting for us to follow his instructions.

I have a friend near Palm Beach, Florida, who owns a restaurant. It's a beautiful place on Lake Worth Pier, one of the longest piers on the Atlantic. When I first met him, I had taken my wife and mother-in-law to eat there, and we were heading out to the pier afterwards. We came around a corner, and this larger-than-life figure says, "Oh my gosh, David Crank! Nicole Crank! I'm Jewish and go to the synagogue, but I watch you on television. I like you, David, and I *love* her. She's way prettier than you!"

So here's this guy, a stranger out in public, who has seen us on television. If we had been in debt like many churches, we could not have been on television at all. But because we maintained discipline and paid off our debt rapidly, we were not paying a bunch of interest to the bank, but investing it in ministry. Because we can afford the air time, we don't have to spend a bunch of time asking our viewers to support the television ministry. In fact, we send out DVDs for free. So our thinking on finances, debt, and ministry investment led to this amazing encounter in this restaurant.

We went out on the pier, and I realized right away that

I liked this guy. I invited him to church, and he actually came and brought some friends. They were like, "I can't believe you're going to church." He said, "No, it isn't a church; it's a school." (We were meeting in a high school at the time, so technically he was right.) We became friends, and a while later we were having lunch when he told me this story.

"Did you hear that my car got stolen last month?"

"No," I answered.

"The craziest thing happened," he said. "After a week they couldn't find the car, so the insurance company gave me a check for my stolen vehicle. But today I got a ticket in the mail from Orlando. Those guys are still driving my car. They drove through the tollway in Orlando with my plates on my car—a stolen vehicle. Can you believe that?!"

I don't know about you, but I think if I planned on driving a stolen car that long, I'd at least change the tags on it! So we laughed about it, and when I was leaving, God gave me something to think about. He said, "Ask the people at your church if they would do that. Then ask them if they're driving a stolen car. Have they used my tithe to buy that car? Is their house littered with stolen things? Are they wearing stolen shoes or clothes?"

Did you know that's possible? Your house could be full of things that are stolen. You may be asking, *When did I steal from God?* That's exactly the question God answered in the Old Testament. He said to his people, "Will a man rob God? Yet you are robbing Me! But you say, 'How have we robbed You?' In tithes and offerings" (Malachi 3:8 NASB).

If you use the first 10 percent for yourself instead of giving it to God, you're driving a stolen car. The *tithe* means *10 percent*. The numerical value of ten. Not two or five or eight. Ten. If you can count to ten, you can count to a million. One, two, three, four, five, six, seven, eight, nine, ten. Start again at one. Eleven, twelve, thirteen . . . Keep these progressions going, and there's strength. God chose a number with power in it. He said, "I want to be first, and I want the first 10 percent. Then I, the Blesser, want to put the blessing on your life. The rest of your life can be blessed, but I must be first."

"A faithful man will abound with blessings, but he who makes haste to be rich will not go unpunished" (Proverbs 28:20 NASB). God wants to bless you as you are faithful first and foremost to him. Oftentimes in America, we try to add blessings to ourselves. We try to get as much we can, can all we get, and sit on our can. Trust me when I tell you there is nothing you can get for yourself that compares to what God has in store for you. There's nothing wrong with being blessed, but there's something very wrong with you being first.

Some of the most blessed people in America are people who love God, and they give back to God. They're charitable. But then there are some people who are just greedy, and they don't share with the needy. It is offensive to God. God said, "You've *robbed* me." That's a strong word.

A couple years ago I was with a friend who doesn't make a lot of money. It's not really going to change God's world whether he tithes or not. He says he doesn't have money to tithe. He goes to this small church in a farming community. He doesn't have money to tithe, but I noticed he had money to buy a new fishing pole. I noticed he had money to buy a hunting knife. He had money to buy boots. But he doesn't have money to tithe.

My friend has never changed financially. He's still broke and barely making it. And I know that God is not a respecter of persons. What God does for other people, he will do for my friend. So don't blame God when you've got things out of order, and he doesn't bless you like you think he should. He's waiting for you to get the sequence right and unlock his blessings.

Through my hunting and fishing friend, God reminded me of the idea of robbing him. I said, "God, how can he rob you? He doesn't have much money anyway." God said, "I won't open up the windows of heaven for him, and I won't change his life so that he can use the extra to impact somebody else's life."

The government is not supposed to feed the poor. It is not supposed to take care of the world. With all of its experts, the government still doesn't even know how to help people. Remember Hurricane Katrina? They could not figure out how to get drinking water to people in New Orleans. They sent down temporary housing that sat in storage lots until it rotted. But I don't really blame them; it is not the politicians' jobs to take care of people. It is the church's job to feed the poor, give water to the thirsty, clothe the naked, and give God the glory. If you were anywhere near the aftermath of the Katrina disaster, that's what you would have seen. Churches opened their doors as shelters, Christians volunteered to give out food and water, and God got the true glory, not the government. We have to put God first. If not, we're stealing from God and robbing the whole nation.

## UNLOCK THE BLESSINGS

In Florida, a businessman friend of mine wanted to buy a $12 million building. He went to look at the building, and while he was inside he heard, "Know this: I always say, 'As many are led by the Spirit of God.'"

He's a tither, believes in the blessing of the Blesser on his life, and listens to me preach all the time. He recognizes that word. It's from Paul's letter to the church in Rome: "For if you live according to the flesh you will die; but if by the Spirit you put to death the deeds of the body, you will live. For as many as are led by the Spirit of God, these are sons of God" (Romans 8:13-14 ESV).

He heard the Spirit tell him, "If it's God today, it's God tomorrow. Just wait." He could have followed his flesh, which wanted the building, but instead he followed the Spirit. This is the inner voice that believers must learn to discern and follow. Jesus said, "My sheep hear my voice, and I know them, and they follow me" (John 10:27 ESV). Some people call it a "hunch" or "intuition," but when we train our ears to hear his Spirit and pursue his peace, it's far more than a "good vibe." It's living a Spirit-led life. God will say things like, "You need to apologize to your mate." He'll tell you when to speak and when to shut up and listen. He wants to guide you, but you have to follow. John Osteen used to say that the Holy Spirit is like a spray of perfume. We have to sense him and go after him to unlock the blessings he has.

This is what my Florida friend did when he heard the Spirit say, "Wait." He waited a whole year. The owners of that building called him back and said, "We've reduced it to $6 million." That's half off in just one year!

So he prayed. And still he heard, "Wait." It would have been easy for his flesh to have said, "See how God blessed me for waiting? Now it's time to buy!" But he knew the importance of *always* being led by the Spirit. And the

Spirit still told him to wait. Those who wait upon the Lord shall renew their strength—their financial strength, marital strength, all of it. If it's God today, it's God tomorrow.

Another year passes, and the bank calls him and says, "Hey, we're willing to sell you this building for what we owe on it."

"What do you owe?" he asked.

"$2 million."

Suddenly, $6 million doesn't sound so great. In one year, my friend couldn't have paid down that note from $6 million to $2 million. Just by waiting (and not making a single payment), he had not only gone from $12 million to half of that, but he saw the price drop almost *85 percent* of its original price. Still, he knew to hear from God before doing anything. So he said, "God, I need a sign to know it's you."

So he went out to the building with the real estate guy who couldn't get the key from the security box to open the building. The real estate guy was fumbling with it, and my friend said, "Let me try. What's the code?"

"Three-five-seven-eight," he replied. My friend couldn't believe the response. He tried the numbers, and the box opened. The key fell into his hand.

"That's my secret code," he said. "I've used that code on every bank card—that's my code! Thank you, God, for the sign!"

When God lines you up for the blessing, he brings the right opportunities into your hands at the right time. He said to his children:

> Blessed shall you be in the city, and blessed shall you be in the country . . . Blessed shall you be when you come in, and blessed shall you be when you go out . . . The LORD will command the blessing on you in your storehouses and in all to which you set your hand, and he will bless you in the land which the LORD your God is giving you . . . The LORD will open to you his good treasure, the heavens, to give the rain to your land in its season, and to bless all the work of your hand. You shall lend to many nations, but you shall not borrow. And the LORD will make you the head and not the tail; you shall be above only, and not be beneath. (Deuteronomy 28:3, 6, 8, 12, 13 NASB)

But wait, there's more. My friend said, "Okay, I'll take the building." Out of the clear blue, a couple of other deals he had forgotten about suddenly came through too. The profits from both of these, neither of which he expected to get, equaled—you guessed it—$2 million. He had been faithful over the "little," so God put him in charge of the "much." There's a line about the Golden Rule being, "Those with the gold rule." But he didn't let "those with the gold" rule over him. He listened to the Spirit, remained faithful and patient, and was rewarded.

I walked through that building going, "Wow, look what the Lord has done!" God's not a respecter of persons. What he did for this businessman, he wants to do for you. But you never come in first by putting God second. And you'll never come in last by putting God first. You must learn to get the sequence of the code right, or you will never unlock your financial future.

You can't save your way out of debt. I'm all for being frugal, wise, and honorable. God said that "those who honor me I will honor" (1 Samuel 2:30 NIV). Solomon, the wisest man in the Bible, said, "Honor the LORD with your wealth and with the best part of everything you produce. Then he will fill your barns with grain, and your vats will overflow with good wine" (Proverbs 3:9-10 NLT). Did you notice the sequence of the code? The "first fruits." Then you will have plenty, and you won't rely on the past because you will continually get "new wine."

Honor the Lord first. If you sow honor, you get honor. If you sow dishonor, you get dishonor. I was at our church down in West Palm Beach, and there was this little watermelon stand on the side of the road that was on the honor system. Piles of watermelons, but nobody there. A sign said that each watermelon was $5, and there was a box. When I lifted open the box, there was cash in it. This is called the honor system. If you're honorable, you take a watermelon or two and put the right amount of money in the box. I know that the man selling the watermelon is honorable because only someone who is honorable assumes that you are honorable. If you are dishonorable, you can take the watermelons and even the cash. But if you don't honor, you will eventually learn honor. You'll learn it like, "Yes, your honor. No, your honor. I'm sorry, your honor. I won't do it again, your honor."

You will never get ahead if you are stealing from God. I hear people all the time say they are "just tithing and trusting God." Of course you should tithe and trust God, but you should also use the brain God gave you! Learn how to be smart. Practice diligence and discipline. Seek wisdom and favor. Be a good steward of what the Master has given you instead of squandering it or burying it in the ground. Until you get that right, ain't nothing going to be right. God wants to honor you, but you must honor him first. This is the code that unlocks his blessings. Don't touch what is his. Put him first. Sow honor. Be blessed.

# CHAPTER 4

## PUTTING THE CURRENT IN CURRENCY

I was teaching financial principles to my son, Austin, and said, "In the morning, before you go to school, how about you make the same amount of money that the big boys make?" And so he got up early in the morning and learned to drive a big Ford Dually, back it up to a forty-foot gooseneck, and drive a bobcat. He made all this dough within a few weeks. He didn't have any bills because he was living for free and eating my food, so before long he had a $1,000.

He saw an old jeep with potential and bought it for like $800. Then he went to work fixing it up. He sanded it down, painted it, and sold it for several *thousand* dollars. He was not even a teenager yet! I told him, "Son, listen to me. This is what you do: Take that money and live life with an open hand. That means stuff needs to come in, and stuff needs to go out. It's called currency."

These are the kinds of lessons we need to be teaching our kids. Train them early so they'll put those lessons into action for a lifetime. Later, Austin had enough money for the down payment on a really nice home. He was still single at the time, so instead of moving into it, he lived with Nicole and me for a while and rented it out. His mortgage was paid by someone else, his house went up in value, and by the time he got married, he had some serious equity and was in a very strong position financially. He avoided the American nightmare of debt and set himself up to live the American Dream while maintaining God's vision of being generous and debt-free.

## BE THE RIVER

Did you ever notice the current in currency? Currency is supposed to flow. When we live with an open hand, we receive, but we also bless. I taught my son what my dad taught me: Put God first through the 10-10-80 principle. The first 10 percent goes to God—period! You don't give him the last 10 percent; you give him the first. He will not come in second, so put him first! And here's a little secret you may not know: When you put God first, you won't come in second. When you put him first, he puts you first.

The next 10 percent goes into savings. Ask any financial expert, and they will tell you that saving something is a necessary part of a smart strategy. Unforeseen expenses pop up, and retirement comes quicker than you can imagine, so start saving now to prevent stress later.

Live off the remaining 80 percent. Too many people live off 110 percent, which lands you in debt. If you budget for 80 percent and stick to it, you will prosper. I would even encourage you to carve out as much as possible from your living expenses for additional giving beyond the tithe.

Our church buys truckloads of blankets. It's cold here in St. Louis. At our campus down in Florida, they don't know anything about this, but $10,000 will buy a whole tractor trailer load of blankets. We take them to the inner city and give them to people who are sleeping outside. We also distribute coats, hats, and gloves for little kids and adults. You'd be surprised how many people are homeless, living on the street. It's really sad. But God has blessed Faith Church in order for us to be a blessing, and we are making a difference. When you live below your means, you can make an even bigger difference in the lives of those in need.

The final vision of the prophet Ezekiel foresees a time when a symbolic river would flow from the temple in Jerusalem. Ezekiel was seeing a picture of Jesus Christ and a new era of mercy, grace, and prosperity. This river of deep, flowing water would bring an abundance of fish to fishermen, a crop of fruitful trees along the banks, and healing to "every living creature" (Ezekiel 47:1-12 NASB). The respected theologian Matthew Henry said that these rivers "signify the gospel of Christ, which went forth from Jerusalem, and spread itself into the countries about, and the gifts and powers of the Holy Ghost which accompanied it, and by virtue of which it spread far and produced strange and blessed effects."[4]

I believe Christians are to be that river. Through the power of the gospel of Christ, we flow blessings to the world. We do this because it is the nature of God. When the Israelites were in the desert after being freed from slavery in Egypt, the Bible says God "opened the rock, and water gushed out; it ran in the dry places like a river" (Psalm 105:41 NASB). Today, the world is a spiritually dry place. It needs God's truth and grace like a desert needs a river. When we put our resources to work, it creates a current that cannot be ignored. Hungry people notice it when Christians feed them. People who need clothes notice it when that church van rolls up and distributes coats and jeans and shoes. Kids dying of diseases from dirty drinking water get a chance at life when a Christian charity drills their village a water well. And when your neighbor has a financial crisis and desperately needs some help, you will be in a position to bless them with what they need when you are debt-free and generous.

How many times have you thought, *Man, I wish I had the money to help?* Well, I have good news for you: God wants you to have the money to help, too! If we will just put God first, listen to the Holy Spirit, and do what he says, we can all be in a better position to help others.

Solomon wrote, "There is one who scatters, and yet increases all the more" (Proverbs 11:24a NASB). The word translated "scatter" also means "disperse." Other Bible translations say "is generous" and "gives freely." Can you believe the wisest man who ever lived (other than Jesus) actually said that whoever gives freely will increase more? Yes, he did!

Then he goes on to contrast the alternative: "another withholds unduly, but comes to poverty" (Proverbs 11:24b NIV). The stingy person just gets poorer. So if you want to be poor, be like Ebenezer Scrooge. If you want to be rich, practice generosity. After all, if you practice it long enough, you'll get pretty good at it!

The next verse in Solomon's lesson illustrates the river principle. "A generous person will prosper; whoever refreshes others will be refreshed" (Proverbs 11:25 NIV). That's the way God is. He likes to give. When we have his heart, we will enjoy giving as well. Now let me give you further revelation. You cannot save your way out of debt, but you can sow your way out of debt. I'm all for saving, as I outlined in the 10-10-80 principle, but it's not the saving that will make you wealthy. It's the one who gives freely who will increase, and it's the generous soul who will be made rich.

When you are a river of God's bounty, he puts the supernatural on your life, and you get an additional raise, an unexpected inheritance, a supernatural opportunity, and other things only God can provide. He can do things no man can do—all kinds of supernatural things that in the natural are impossible. The Lord asked Abraham, and later Jeremiah, this question: Is there anything too hard for me? (Genesis 18:14, Jeremiah 32:27) He is asking you that same question today. The answer, of course, is no. With God all things are possible. Giving is the best way, not getting. Your generosity begets his generosity.

## BLESSED TO BLESS

Some friends and I were in a restaurant one day, and the service was horrible. We couldn't even get our order taken. So I caught the attention of the waitress and pulled out a twenty-dollar bill. "This isn't your tip," I said. "This is an advance on your tip."

I just wanted some food, but this young woman almost started crying. We found out that she was having a hard time paying her bills and worrying about the upcoming Christmas season and what she could buy her kids, if anything. I pulled out a hundred bucks and gave it to her.

So did four other people at our table. Obviously, we got the best service ever after that! But more importantly, we ended up praying with her, and it changed her life. That's what money is for—not just getting what we want or need, but using it to impact lives for God's glory.

Generosity is a great virtue, but it's not a virtue without purpose. Now that you understand that God wants to bless you, it's important to know that a big reason he wants to bless you is so that you can be a blessing to other people. And you can't do that if you don't have any money. Scripture says you can't serve God and money, which is absolutely true. But you can serve God *with* money. Here's one of the reasons why. "Remember the words of the LORD Jesus, that He said, 'It is more blessed to give than to receive'" (Acts 20:35 WBT).

It's kind of funny how we think we want to be blessed and, at the same time, get stuff. Yes, it's great to get stuff. It's a blessing for sure. But Jesus said if you want to be even more blessed, be the giver! Have you ever given away something and thought, *Oh that felt good?* It's an amazing feeling to give something away and be more blessed than the person you gave it to. Why does it work this way? Because one person receives the gift, which is awesome, but the one giving the gift gets God's blessing for being the giver. When you sow into the kingdom, you don't just get *a* return—you get a thirty, sixty, and *hundred-fold* return.

Our church had saved up enough for a down payment on a new building when I felt like God was instructing us to give it to another church. We did it. Within three months, we had been given even more than what we had given away. We received the blessing because we were obedient and generous with what God entrusted to us. When God asks you to do something that's not natural, it's because it's supernatural. It's like that farmer who sows a seed in his field. He doesn't just get the same amount of seed back; he gets a booming crop. So being a giver does good, feels good, and reaps a great reward.

One Halloween the son of one of our campus pastors was giving out candy, and he ran out. This little bitty guy went into his personal stash to get more, and his mom said, "What are you doing?" He said, "People keep coming, and I gotta give them candy." She said, "But that's your candy." He replied, "I don't care. I'm having fun giving it to them."

He got it! Even as a kid, he got a taste of being blessed by being a giver. I love this story because this is the heart of Nicole and me, which extends to our whole church. We love to bless others by giving to them. We go to the inner city and give people blankets, clothes, food, and more. We partner with other Christian organizations like The Dream Center and Hand of Hope to reach beyond our own city. Our church gives away 10 percent of our income, and we sow on top of that. We are qualified for God's blessings because we have the sequence in order, and that's why Faith Church has experienced such explosive growth. We don't have a poverty mentality; we have a giving mentality. We don't just say, "God bless us." We say, "God, let us bless others!"

We love Haiti and the Haitian people so much that we will go over there and take teams from our church just to find a way to bless them. I was there not too long ago sleeping with lizards the size of alligators running across the bed. My little daughter, Ashtyn, was a little freaked out about that, but she loves the Haitian kids and wants to be a blessing to them. They're literally starving to death. It's so bad that we've seen them eating dirt. And the idea of toys—that's something they've never seen.

The last time we left, Ashtyn said, "Dad, they're just playing with rocks. Can we build them a playground?"

"They've never even seen a playground," I told her. "I don't even know how we would do it."

She said, "We can do it! I'll give you my life savings!"

She came home and gave us her life savings. The playground was $25,000, and she was $24,900 short! That's why we need to be blessed. It's not enough to *want* to help others; we need to have the money to be *able* to help others. People need food, clothing, medicine, shelter, drinking water, and occasionally, a playground. We get in the habit of settling for a prayer that says, "God help them some-how." I believe we should be praying, "God enable me to help them in Your name!"

It was such a blessing to build more than a simple playground in Haiti. We built a full recreation area with fencing, a playground, and much more. And then it was so great, we built another one. Both of them cost money. That's why we need it. It is worth noting that the $50,000 it cost for those two playgrounds came out of the money we saved by paying off debt quickly. Instead of giving the money to the banks, we used it to bless the poor in Jesus' name! When we honor God with our finances and obey the Spirit in our actions, we can do amazing things for his kingdom. As I am writing this book, we just sent a check for $48,000 to Haiti for a medical vehicle.

> **AND WHEN YOU ENTER THE LAND OF PLENTY AND REALLY START TO PROSPER, YOU WON'T BELIEVE THE AMAZING THINGS YOU CAN DO.**

You probably have dreams for God's kingdom. Maybe you want to build a church, establish an outreach, or bless a needy family. If you're a child of the King, then I know you have a desire to be generous. Whatever it is that God has placed on your heart, know that it is on his heart too. Once you leave the Land of Lack and enter the Land of Even, you can start to do these things that God has put inside you. And when you enter the Land of Plenty and really start to prosper, you won't believe the amazing things you can do. Freedom is powerful thing, and financial freedom enables you to be a huge blessing to others.

God is able to bless you. Don't doubt it. It's all over his Word. Not only can he do it, but he *wants* to do it so that he can do more through you. There are several variations of an old saying that goes something like this: "Without God, we can do nothing. But without us, he will not do everything." In other words, he is waiting on us to be his "hands and feet"—to reach out and carry his truth, love, and mercy to others.

Skeptics often ask, "Why doesn't God just fix every problem in the world?" I think the answer is the same as the answer to the question, "Why doesn't God just save everyone in the world himself?" The last thing Jesus told his followers before he ascended to the right hand of the Father was this: "Go therefore and make disciples of all the nations, baptizing them in the name of the Father and of the Son and of the Holy Spirit, teaching them to observe all things that I have commanded you" (Matthew 28:19-20 ESV).

Why doesn't God make everyone his disciple? Because he told *us* to. There's a whole other discussion about free will and natural revelation in there, but you get my point.

We are commanded to go. As the body of Christ, we have a role in reaching out to share the gospel, and one of the best ways to open the door of people's hearts is to meet their basic needs.

James, the half-brother of Jesus, wrote, "Pure and undefiled religion before God the Father is this: to visit orphans and widows in their distress, and refusing to let the world corrupt you" (James 1:27 NLT). You are called to be a holy helper! To do that, you need the means.

Jesus said, "For I was hungry, and you fed me. I was thirsty, and you gave me a drink. I was a stranger, and you invited me into your home. I was naked, and you gave me clothing. I was sick, and you cared for me. I was in prison, and you visited me." How do we do that to Jesus? He answered, "I tell you the truth, when you did it to one of the least of these my brothers and sisters, you were doing it to me!" (Matthew 25:35-36, 40 NLT). So you might have enough money for you, but do have enough money to feed the poor? Can you afford to take in someone in need? Can you fund a prison ministry?

You may be thinking, *No, I can't really do any of that right now.* So what *can* you do? God starts by asking you to do what you can do and then enables you to do what you can't.

Jesus told a story about money and finished with these points: "He who is faithful in a very little is also faithful in much" and "if you have not been faithful in that which is another's, who will give you that which is your own?" (Luke 16:10-12 ESV).

You're never going to get anywhere by waiting on more. You have to start by being faithful with whatever you have. You will eventually be able to bless big, but you have to start by blessing others while you have little. When you realize that you are blessed to bless and put it into practice, you begin to develop the habits and the mindset that puts you in a position to be trusted with more.

## BUILD THE KINGDOM

Many of the top supporters of our church didn't have any money when they started attending. We certainly didn't have any millionaires when we started. We just raised up our own by teaching them the principle of putting God first.

One man began to put God first in the area of his business. He grew from two employees to 300. God did something absolutely crazy in his life and blessed him big time. In retirement, he decided that he wanted to help start our church in Palm Beach. He knew I wouldn't go on television in Palm Beach if the bill wasn't paid because I didn't ask for money on television, so he took the initiative. He said, "We're going to pay all the television bills." They put us on FOX 29. It blew up so big that ABC wanted us. Soon we were on ABC, NBC, CBS, and FOX, and one individual paid the bill every month because God re-sourced him so much.

You might be thinking, *That can't happen to me.* I doubt my friend at church ever thought he could do that either, but he did. He honored God, God honored him, and he put his blessings back to work. He received, and he gave. He kept the current going. Now we have a campus in Flor-ida, and hundreds of thousands of lives have been changed because one man understood the power of obedience.

God can take you from a place of desperation and put you right into your wealthy place. Oftentimes he does it rapidly. You might be thinking it's getting too late. Lis-ten, when you bless it, break it, give it to God, and say, "You're first," he can do things that make people scratch their heads in wonder. If you bless God, he will bless you.

Christians are real big on quoting a couple of Scriptures. First, "I can do all things through Christ who strengthens me" (Philippians 4:13 KJ21). Next, "God will supply all your needs according to His riches in glory" (Philippians 4:19 NASB). Those are good ones, right? Problem is, they can be really misunderstood and used out of context.

First, you have to look at the setting in which Paul said those things. He was writing to the church at Philippi, ba-sically saying, "No one else helped me in the gospel min-istry. Nobody else supplied our needs. Nobody else was tithing and giving to our organization. I was dirt poor, and you were too. But you did whatever you could, and God is going to bless you for it."

Evidently, the people at the church in Philippi were taking care of Paul for a while, but they fell on hard times and were not able to for a while. Paul never complained, even in his need. He "learned both to be full and be hungry." How many of us would be content while we were hungry? It's easy when we're full, but Paul said that even while he was hungry and needy, his strength was Christ. He could do all things not because he was strong, but because Christ in him gave him strength.

Then he says the Philippians joined him in his distress. They suffered with him. Even when he wasn't ministering to them, they supported him. He didn't ask them for help; he only sought the fruit that came from him being able to share the gospel. But through a mutual friend, Paul received the gift from the Philippians. His necessities were covered, and he rejoiced. Then he declared that their needs would be met because they had blessed him. They didn't just sow out of their abundance; they also sowed out of their distress. Paul spoke a word of blessing over them, and it wasn't "God will supply my needs." It was "God will supply *your* need" (Philippians 4:10-20).

When we remain faithful and support God's kingdom work, even when we ourselves may be in hard times, our needs, like the church in Philippi, will be met by God.

Why? For his glory, not our own. And don't forget your part in his plan. Those suggestions in chapter 2 are steps you must take to demonstrate your faithfulness in managing what God has entrusted to you. Paul was faithful and had his needs met. The church in Philippi was faithful, and God promised to meet their need. You must be faithful in order to fulfill your expectation that God will supply your needs.

If you want to be blessed, be a blessing to others; then give God the glory. A lot of people claim the promise, but they never read the verses around it. With no seed, there is no harvest. With no risk, there is no reward. There comes a point in your life when you have to trust God with all your heart, lean not on your own understanding, acknowledge him in all of your ways, and let him direct your path (Proverbs 3:5-6). What I'm saying is that you will be at the right place at the right time meeting the right people because you serve the right God. He will take care of you in grand style. We just have to say, "Here it is. I don't have much. But what I have is yours. I will use what you have given me to build your kingdom."

One day a man walked down the aisle of church and introduced himself. He was wearing a pair of cut-off shorts and a sleeveless shirt. A pack of cigarettes was hanging out, and he said, "Nice to meet you. You're one hell of a preacher." I thought, *Doesn't he know you're not supposed to cuss in church?* But I simply said, "Thank you."

We talked, and as I was listening to him, I was drawn to him. I set a goal to go after his soul and help him. I suggested we go to lunch some time, and he agreed, so I took his number down. A few days later, we went to lunch. He pulled up in a junked-up truck—he was just a good ol' boy who needed Jesus. We talked about things we both enjoy, like motorcycles and horses, and he invited me to his place to look at his horses. So I went over to his barn, and all of a sudden, I saw all these Taco Bell trucks. I asked him what kind of business he was in, and he said he owned a bunch of Taco Bell and Kentucky Fried Chicken franchises. I thought, *God is going to bless this man.*

He started coming to the church right about the time we needed to buy the bar. Someone had converted it to an indoor go-cart track, and in order for us to use it as a church, 1.2 million pounds of asphalt had to be taken out. It was going to cost hundreds of thousands of dollars to dispose of all that. I took him over to the building, and he walked around there looking at it and said he didn't think it should cost so much. He called a guy that worked on his franchises and told him about the job. And you know what? He paid for every bit of that to be removed and hauled off. He hadn't given his life to Christ yet, but he wanted to help the church.

A few weeks later we were on a trip together, and my

new friend began to talk about his mom, saying she had gone to heaven. I began to talk to him about heaven, and right there in that hotel room he gave his life to Jesus. A few days later we were on his dad's boat, and not long after that, his dad gave his life to the Lord.

My friend and his family have been some of our strongest supporters over the years, helping us preach the gospel all over the world. God didn't ask his dad to sell his yacht. He didn't ask my friend to sell his fast food franchises. Instead, God blessed them as they put him first. I believe God is waiting to bless a lot of people like them. For so long the church world has been known as "busted and disgusted," and out in the world nobody is asking about how good God is. If we will learn to honor him and put his currency in motion, though, it will wake people up to his goodness and grace.

One day Jesus was teaching when he dropped this nugget of revelation on them: "Do not lay up for yourselves treasures on earth, where moth and rust destroy and where thieves break in and steal; but lay up for yourselves treasures in heaven, where neither moth nor rust destroys and where thieves do not break in and steal. For where your treasure is, there your heart will be also" (Matthew 6:19-21 ESV). In your quest to get a bigger house, nicer car, or even the latest iPhone, are you putting any treasure in heaven? How do we even do that? It's not like there's a

First Bank of Heaven down the street where you can directly deposit your paycheck. The answer is that we work to build the kingdom of heaven.

When Jesus was being questioned by Pilate, he affirmed his kingship but clearly separated himself from earthly kings when he said, "My kingdom is not of this world" (John 18:36 ESV). So how do earthly dollars translate to heavenly treasure? By sowing into kingdom work. When we use our physical resources to advance his spiritual kingdom, we "lay up treasures in heaven." The return on that investment isn't subject to the whims of financial markets; it is gold for eternity. That's what our media investor in Florida did for years. And even before he got saved, Mike was investing in it too. Soon, his heart followed his treasure, and he became an heir in Christ's kingdom.

There is no better place to put your money than God's investment portfolio. When we are generous, bless others, and build his kingdom, the flow of blessings goes through us to the world, changing lives along the way. That currency in that river not only brings hope and healing to the lost, but also joy and satisfaction to us.

# CHAPTER 5

## INTO THE DEEP

I want to change your thinking about finances, your business, and your life. This mind-blowing truth is found in the Gospel of Luke:

> On one occasion, while the crowd was pressing in on him to hear the word of God, he was standing by the lake of Gennesaret, and he saw two boats by the lake, but the fishermen had gone out of them and were washing their nets. Getting into one of the boats, which was Simon's, he asked him to put out a little from the land. And he sat down and taught the people from the boat. And when he had finished

speaking, he said to Simon, "Put out into the deep and let down your nets for a catch." And Simon answered, "Master, we toiled all night and took nothing! But at your word I will let down the nets." And when they had done this, they enclosed a large number of fish, and their nets were breaking. They signaled to their partners in the other boat to come and help them. And they came and filled both the boats, so that they began to sink. (Luke 5:1-7 ESV)

The picture at the beginning of this story is pretty amazing. Jesus Christ, the worker of miracles who had caused such a stir that "multitudes" were following him around, was there by a lake. People were pressing in, hoping he would speak. But what are these fishermen doing? They are washing their nets. It's all business as usual for these guys. Sure, there's this Messiah dude about to talk to a crowd of people, but they had things that needed tending. They had to wash their nets. (Sounds like a bit of an excuse, like, "I'd love to, but I gotta wash my nets." I guess if you're a fisherman for a living, it's legit. Anyway, back to the story.)

Jesus was about to talk to the crowd, but more importantly, he was about to blow the minds of these fishermen.

But first he had a couple of things that needed to be done. They needed some fish, and he was about to deliver—scratch that—he was about to *over*-deliver. He had to lay down some groundwork first, though.

That's what I want to do with you. I believe God wants to over-deliver his blessings to you very soon, but some groundwork of truth needs to be laid down so you know exactly who is to get the glory here. (Hint: It's not you.) You also need to change the way you look at things. I'm afraid you may be too busy washing your nets to notice what Jesus wants to do, so take a break from the mundane for a moment and see if maybe your life is about to radically change.

## CHRIST IN YOUR BOAT

Look at that line, "Then he got into one of the boats, which was Simon's, and asked him to put out a little from the land." I don't know what Jesus said to Simon (who would later be called Peter) to convince him to be the one to lend his boat, but when Jesus asked, Simon complied. I can picture this surly, outdoorsy fisherman-type rinsing off his nets when this Jewish teacher walks up and says, "Hey, can I borrow your boat so I can preach?" He could see the crowd. He no doubt had heard the commotion. He probably wasn't in a great mood since he'd caught nothing all day. But he said, "Fine. Get in my small-business enterprise, my livelihood, my ability to eat, and pay the mortgage."

And that's the key.

Have you invited Jesus Christ into your "boat?" Have you said, "Here, take center stage in my job and my finances." If you really think about it, there could have been a rush to get to Jesus that could have crushed the fishing vessel. Or an angry mob of Pharisees could have taken their wrath out on Simon and boycotted his business for helping this man they considered a dangerous religious zealot. Or the Roman government could have decided that what Jesus was doing was illegal and confiscated Simon's boat for helping him. Really, there were many ways things that could have gone wrong by letting Jesus in his boat.

Right now in America, and even in the rest of the world, there's a massive push to get Jesus out of the workplace. People literally say that if you choose to honor Christ in your business, you should not be able to run it. They'd rather have you on welfare than contributing to society. They have twisted the words in a letter Thomas Jefferson wrote to pretend there is some wall between church and state that precludes you from honoring God in any place except your home or your congregation. But God never intended to be the Lord of your privacy. He is the God of the marketplace just as much as he is the God of the sanctuary.

Don't get me wrong. Putting Jesus in your business doesn't mean you have to put a giant cross on your pizza parlor. You don't even need to put a little fish symbol on your business card. That may be nice, but it's frankly not enough. You have to put God right in the middle of all your business practices. That will seriously change the way you do business.

Paul wrote, "Whatever you do, do it heartily, as to the LORD and not to men, knowing that from the LORD you will receive the reward of the inheritance; for you serve the LORD Christ" (Colossians 3:23-24 AKJV). To the church in Ephesus, he instructed them to work not "as men-pleasers, but as bondservants of Christ, doing the will of God from the heart, with goodwill doing service, as to the LORD, and not to men" (Ephesians 6:6-7). When Jesus is in the middle of our boat, we will work more diligently, honestly, happily, and, as we will soon see, fruitfully.

The same is true when we put him in the center of our finances. Christ in your boat means inviting him into the way you do work as well as how you manage the rewards of your work. As I've said, if Christ isn't Lord of all, he isn't Lord at all. With Jesus in Simon's boat, Simon's world was about to change. That was the first step to the miracle he needed, and it is the first step to every breakthrough in your life.

There is a girl I grew up in church with. She graduated from high school but didn't have the money to go to college. However, she was very talented and loved God.

She applied at a large, worldwide bank and got the job. They promoted her up and up until she earned a six-figure salary. Despite her earned success, she was always nervous that people would find out she hadn't gone to college and decide she was unqualified. This is how the devil works, always whispering fear on the inside. But she chose to trust God. She told herself, *I have this position because God put me here. My credentials don't qualify. My education doesn't qualify. But if God qualifies me, then I am qualified.*

She worked at the bank for many years until one day they suddenly and unexpectedly laid her off. They said they had to eliminate her position entirely but would give her six months of severance pay. She came to church and told Nicole and me what happened. We were sad with her. We thought it was over.

For the first month, she unsuccessfully looked for another job that paid the same. By month three, she was just looking for something close. She started worrying. That turned to fear by month five, and with thirty days left, she started freaking out. She had Jesus in her boat, but as the disciples discovered, storms still happened.

> Now it came to pass on a certain day, that
> he went into a ship with his disciples: and

> he said unto them, Let us go over unto the
> other side of the lake. And they launched
> forth. But as they sailed he fell asleep: and
> there came down a storm of wind on the
> lake; and they were filled with water, and
> were in jeopardy. (Luke 8:22-23 KJV)

This is where my friend was. She was cruising along doing God's will, crossing from this side to that side. Jesus was in her boat, but a storm still came. She did what she could, but it was as if Jesus was asleep. She started to panic. Her inability put her in jeopardy.

> And they came to him, and awoke him,
> saying, "Master, master, we perish." Then
> he arose, and rebuked the wind and the
> raging of the water: and they ceased, and
> there was a calm. And he said unto them,
> "Where is your faith?" And they being
> afraid wondered, saying one to anoth-
> er, "What manner of man is this! for he
> commandeth even the winds and water,
> and they obey him." (Luke 8:24-25 KJV)

A few days before her compensation ran out, the bank called her back. They said, "We need you back." They apologized for laying her off and offered her a promotion, a bonus, and even an assistant. Plus, she wouldn't lose any seniority. Later she told me, "I wish I hadn't wasted six months. I should've enjoyed my time off!"

Putting Jesus in your boat doesn't mean you won't ever experience a storm. But it does mean that your faith will be tested. The good news is that you have the assurance that Jesus will never leave you or forsake you. He will provide every need. And he commands the winds and the water. So when the storm comes, he will either ride it out with you or speak the word to calm things down. You may be a little seasick, but you never need to wonder if he is in control. He always is.

The God of the breakthrough will come into your life and give you a promotion, a raise, a change in that situation, a miracle, or whatever else you need. But you have to learn to trust God. You will never see what's on the other side of your fear until you sail out and say, "God, I know the plans you have for me, and they're for good." And he goes, "Yeah, I do have plans for you. But you need to pass a couple tests. But don't fear, I'm right here in the boat with you, and I've got everything under control."

## STRETCH YOUR MIND

After Jesus got in Simon's boat, he taught the crowd. You have to wonder what was going through this fisherman's mind. There he was—a captive audience sitting right next to the Son of God giving divine revelation. If he wasn't blowing his mind, Jesus was at least stretching it a lot. When he finished, he said to Simon, "Launch out into the deep."

God wants you to launch into new territories in business as well as your personal life, but you will never do it if you do not change your mindset. A mind stretched never goes back to its original size. If you're the smartest person at the table, you're at the wrong table. As your life begins to grow, your mind begins to expand, especially when it comes to the way you think about God's blessings. When you can change the way you think, you can change the way you live.

Simon and the other fishermen had worked all night and caught nothing. If you've ever fished, you know how frustrating that is. For these guys, it was even worse than that. Fishing was their livelihood, so it was a financial disaster as well. But right in the middle of Simon's trouble, God was building his faith. The Bible says, "faith comes by hearing, and hearing by the word of Christ" (Romans 10:17 NHEB). So Simon's faith had to have been expanding when Jesus said, "Launch out into the deep."

He pointed out that he and the other fishermen had worked really hard and caught nothing. It's the same day, it's the same boat, it's the same nets, it's the same people.

What has changed? Duh! Jesus is in the boat, right?

Still, Simon called his business partners, James and John, and they went out. This time when they threw out their nets, they caught so much that their nets began to break, and their boats began to sink. A single boat could even not contain it, and then they began to yell to all their friends on the shore. They all began profiting from Jesus' blessing. They were yelling, "Come on, everybody, get your boats out here right now!" All of their ships began to fill up because God is not a broke God. He does exceedingly and abundantly above all we could ever ask or think.

When Jesus gets on your boat, he will tell you to launch out into the deep for a great haul, pressed down, shaken together, running over. He will cause good things to happen to you, but you have to listen to him! You can't say, "Jesus, this is my business, just stay on the shore," and you can't stick to the shallows when he says to launch into the deep. You have to know his voice and obey if you want to be stretched.

I would not have bought a campus worth an estimated $21 million if my mind hadn't been stretched. Or another campus valued at $37 million. I grew up in a trailer. I thought in small terms. I'm not qualified to do all the things God has led me to do for his kingdom, but he took me into deeper waters, past my education and qualifications. He moved me way past where I came from because his plans are not based on where we come from, but rather on where he is going. With him in our boat, we go too.

Promotion doesn't come from the east or the west; promotion comes from God. Blessing doesn't come from what we do; it comes from what he wants to do. We just need to get in the right position, hear his voice, and go where he tells us to go. We don't serve the God of the shallows; we serve the God of the deep.

Zerubbabel was the head of the tribe of Judah after the Northern Kingdom had fallen to the Babylonians and the temple at Jerusalem was destroyed. He was the quarterback of the losing team, so much so that he was referred to as "the prince of the captivity." But God had big plans for him. He was about to turn their losing season around.

God moved the heart of Cyrus, the king of Persia, following Jeremiah's prophecy that the temple would be rebuilt and restored. Cyrus called on the Israelites saying, "The LORD, the God of heaven, has given me all the kingdoms of the earth and He has appointed me to build Him a house in Jerusalem, which is in Judah. Whoever there is among you of all His people, may his God be with him! Let him go up to Jerusalem which is in Judah and rebuild the house of the LORD, the God of Israel; He is the God who is in Jerusalem" (Ezra 1:2-3 NASB).

Zerubbabel answered the call. He launched into the

deep and with great fanfare laid the foundation for the new, restored temple of God. Then he ran into trouble. He had opposition from the Samaritans, and the Israelites got busy building themselves nice houses. For sixteen years, the work on the temple stood idle. They had laid the foundation, but they didn't finish.

When you launch into the deep, you will face opposition. The devil doesn't want you to complete your destiny. He can't win, but he can throw some opposition. He will whisper lies to you, telling you that you aren't qualified, aren't blessed, aren't called, and so on. You will also face temptation to get sidetracked. You might get comfortable in your success. You might even be tempted to think that all the fish are a result of your skill and hard work, even though you had nothing until Jesus got in your boat. Just know that God will not share his glory with any man—even you!

> **THE DEVIL DOESN'T WANT YOU TO COMPLETE YOUR DESTINY.**

If you start to take credit for your success, you're sunk. If you balk at the wind and the waves, you'll never reach your destination.

Such was the case with Zerubbabel for those long years. He may have forgotten about God's work, but God hadn't. He raised up a prophet, Zechariah, and gave him this powerful word: "Not by might nor by power, but by my Spirit" (Zechariah 4:6 NIV).

When you're in the deep, remember that you are in over your head! You will not succeed by your own strength. You will not haul in a great catch by your own power. It is only by his Spirit!

God continued to speak through Zechariah, instructing the distracted leader: "The hands of Zerubbabel have laid the foundation of this temple; his hands will also complete it" (Zechariah 4:9 NIV).

Do you hear that? God will finish the work he has started. He wants you to finish with him. Zechariah's word sparked a fire in Zerubbabel, and he finished rebuilding the temple, fulfilling Jeremiah's prophecy and setting the stage for the arrival of the Messiah. It was hard work, but God's hand was on it, so it could not fail.

Once you've set out for deeper waters, complete the job! When you feel like you can't do it on your own, take comfort in the fact that you are not on your own. When you are at your lowest, having worked all night and caught nothing, understand that in your weakness, God is strong. As he told Paul, "My grace is sufficient for you, for my power is made perfect in weakness" (2 Corinthians 12:9 ESV).

As was the case with Simon Peter, we can't make fish bite. (Ask any fisherman who has tried!) As was the case with Zerubbabel, we can't control what governments do. We can only hear and obey, which enables us to do more than what comes natural. It's supernatural. God's plan for you goes beyond the shallow things you can accomplish on your own.

## THROW OUT YOUR NET

So you've got Jesus in your boat, you've launched out into the deep, and you're wondering what to do next. For Simon, it was "let down your nets." There's no special hidden meaning in that. Simon didn't need a theological degree to decipher it or a high-profile preacher to explain it. That's language a fisherman understood. Even so, his mind argued against it.

"Master, we have toiled all night and caught nothing," he said. How many times have you felt the Holy Spirit telling you do something, and your first reaction was "Yeah, but . . ." That's what Simon thought. *We know how to fish. We tried all night. It won't work!*

Still, something was stirring in his soul. His faith had grown, and his mind had stretched because of the truth Jesus had spoken. So after his "but," he said, "*nevertheless, at your word I will let down the net.*"

That's the final key to unlock the blessings. When God says to do something, act on it. Like Simon Peter, you only need to do one thing: obey. Trust me, it will fill your boat and even break your nets.

You might be reading right now, and you lost your job,

your house, your car, and your dog. There are two things you need to do: First, listen to some country music, rewind it, and then get your dog back. Second, you gotta get to a church that preaches the Word and says, "No weapon forged against you will prevail" (Isaiah 54:17 NIV).

When my dad went on to be with the Lord, God asked Nicole and me to sell everything we owned. We had a great house and a beautiful place. Nicole was the top salesperson in a successful telecommunications business. We were doing very well and having a great time, but when my dad died the Lord spoke to me and said, "Would you give that to me? Will you ask Nicole to be a volunteer at the church? Will you sell everything you own?"

I was kind of like the rich young ruler. I walked away sad. But then God spoke to me again and said, "You will look back on your life and regret the fact that you didn't give everything to me." To make a long story short, we sold our house, gave our stuff away, and moved into a small subdivision southwest of St. Louis. Not long after starting Faith Church, we experienced 13 percent growth *every week*. That means every Sunday, we had to set out 13 percent more chairs than we did the previous week. The building filled up within a couple months. Then I was doing not one service, but two, then three, four, five, six, seven, even eight. It was brutal. But then it was like God looked at me and said, "Now, I'm going to trust you with much."

He gave us the biggest bar in the state of Missouri. We meet at what was once called "In Cahoots." Thousands of people who had been partying and drinking knew where to go! Instead of pointing a judgmental finger in their faces, we pointed them to Christ. Instead of slapping them in the face, we welcomed them with open arms. And guess what? Thousands of people got saved, and Faith Church exploded. We went on television. We opened new campuses. And never once have I regretted obeying God. Nicole and I trusted him, and he blessed us. He wants to do the same for you. You probably won't turn a bar into a church, but God wants to do something great in your life.

That nagging insecurity and guilt goes away when you just obey. God wants to make you prosperous in him, regardless of whether you are "abased or abound" by the world's measure. It's the same as it was in the days of the Old Testament in that "the eyes of the LORD run to and fro throughout the whole earth, to show himself strong in the behalf of them whose heart is perfect toward him" (2 Chronicles 16:9 KJ21).

When you trust God with all your heart, he doesn't send you out to let you down. He doesn't send you into the deep unless he has something for you to do. And when you obey, you are guaranteed to succeed. So don't worry, don't wonder, and don't waiver. Listen and obey.

Cast all your cares upon him for he cares for you. He's watching over you like a little sparrow (Matthew 10:31, Luke 12:7). You don't see the sparrows running around going, "I don't know what we're going to do today. It's so hot out here today. I don't know if God can supply water." He always supplies the resources the birds need. The monkeys in the Panama Canal are jumping from tree to tree today with tens of thousands of extra bananas. God didn't get the memo that there's waste. He's saying, "I've got more than enough. I can take care of you, and your mom, and your kids, and your children's children. And you'll have enough left over to leave an inheritance."

I was praying a while back when God said to me, "Read the book of Acts on your knees." So I began to read it and reread it every day, praying and crying for the Lord to show me what he was trying to communicate. A few months later, as I was reading about how Paul and Silas were in jail and sang praises at midnight and were freed along with the other prisoners, I heard the Lord say, "I want you to buy some late-night time slots in West Palm Beach, Florida, and St. Louis to preach the gospel to people who are imprisoned in the middle of the night." God miraculously provided the funds to buy the time, and we went on the air all throughout the night. We spread a message of hope, telling people that no matter how dark it gets, if you will sing his praises in the middle of the night, you will be freed. Every trial has an expiration date. Like milk, it has a shelf life. The Enemy cannot maintain an attack. You need to hear with your own ears and believe with all your heart that God is about to bring net-breaking, ship-sinking, supernatural opportunity that only he can bring because he is your source. The message was heard. The lost were saved, people's lives were changed, and God got the glory.

One guy who saw our program and was impacted by the gospel owns a television network on Dish and DirecTV. It didn't have any religious programming—at least not until he saw our program. He was moved by the Spirit to put us on his network right in the middle of secular programming and has never charged us a dime! So now we're not just reaching the Palm Beach area; we're also reaching the entire country and beyond. It's all because we sought the Lord, obeyed the Spirit, and continue living by his principles.

I grew up with a buddy of mine. He was a tither, paycheck to paycheck. God got the first fruits. He and his wife used to raise livestock, and each time they would sell a cow, their little boy would bring in a check with the first 10 percent from the sale. They lived it, and they taught their son. God blessed Abraham because he taught his children and his children's children. My buddy did that too.

I have another friend who was born again watching

our church on television. I introduced the two to each other. One day one of them said to our friend and me, "I'd love if you guys got a couple days off sometime to fly down to Miami in my single-engine airplane, rent some motorcycles, and drive to the Florida Keys."

I had never done that seven-mile bridge, and I love motorcycles, so you know I was interested. We finally made the trip happen and had a great time. On the way back, we were in the plane (and it was so slow we were telling the geese, "Go around!"), and I'm in the co-pilot seat as our buddy's leaning in from the back. His head was between us, and he was talking about his dreams—how he wished he could do this and that, but he couldn't because people wouldn't let him. He was living paycheck to paycheck and blah, blah, blah. And I'm like, "What's up, man? You got gifts. You got talents. You're a tither. You're a giver. You're at the right table." I told my other friend, "I don't know anything about writing business plans, but he needs to figure out how to get a loan and build his own business."

Our friend said, "Okay, I'll help him." A couple of days later, they wrote up a business plan. Within a few more days, my friend called and said, "You won't believe it, but I have a couple people fighting over this. They want to invest in my business."

So they did it.

Within one year, most businesses fail. Our friend's, the tither, blew up. He started his business in Springfield, Missouri. It went so big that he was able to buy the original investors out. Year two, it got so big that they were one of the biggest in America. Year three, they were one of the biggest in the world. My buddy was living the life of his dreams in only three short years because he put God first, launched out, and lived in obedience.

I'm talking to you. God's going to turn this thing around for your good. Just don't freak out. Know that it's a word from God that he's speaking through me to you. Trust him. Will you trust him? Jesus said to his disciples, "With men it is impossible, but not with God; for all things are possible with God" (Mark 10:27 KJ21). He was talking about the rich young ruler who couldn't let go of his self-made wealth to truly follow Christ. He was talking about the one who served money, rather than letting his money serve God. Because he wouldn't let Jesus in his boat, right in the middle of his money-making means, his situation looked hopeless. That man kept all the rules, but he couldn't enter into God's kingdom here on earth because he wouldn't let go, trust, and obey.

I'm inviting you to step into the impossible in the natural by giving up control and letting God make it possible in the supernatural. Your way will never work, but God's way will never fail. Now that you've heard the truth, it's time to act. Don't think, *I can't do it*, because it's not about you. It's about God, and he can absolutely do it. So listen to the Holy Spirit, live in obedience, and prepare to let God prosper you according to his terms and his timeline. That's his promise, so that's your guarantee.

# ENDNOTES

1. Matt Phillips, "The Long Story of U.S. Debt, From 1790 to 2011, in One Little Chart," *The Atlantic*, November 13, 2012, http://www.theatlantic.com/business/archive/2012/11/the-long-story-of-us-debt-from-1790-to-2011-in-1-little-chart/265185/.

2. Dave Boyer, "$20 Trillion Man: National Debt Nearly Doubles During Obama Presidency," *Washington Times*, November 1, 2015, http://www.washingtontimes.com/news/2015/nov/1/obama-presidency-to-end-with-20-trillion-national-/.

3. Robert Harrow, "Average Credit Card Debt in America: 2016 Facts and Figures," *Value Penguin*, November 28,2016, http://www.valuepenguin.com/average-credit-card-debt.

4. Henry, Matthew. *An Exposition of All the Books of the Old and New Testament*. Berwick-upon-Tweed: Gracie, 1809. Print.

# ABOUT DAVID CRANK

David Crank is the founder and senior pastor of Faith-Church.com, spanning four different campuses including three campuses in Saint Louis, Missouri, and one in West Palm Beach, Florida. Faith Church is a place where "people connect, families grow, and lives are changed." Pastor David has a passion for making the complex simple by spreading God's love to people in fun and relevant ways they can understand and apply to their everyday lives. When his father passed away, he took his church from 200 members to now 18,000 active members.

Pastor David has been privileged to minister to a large global audience where he uses his motivational humor and inspirational whit while speaking at conferences and churches around the world. He is also a frequent guest on some of the biggest Christian television networks.

He and his wife, Nicole, together share their time between the Sunshine State and the Show-Me State along with their daughter, Ashtyn. Their son, Austin, and their daughter-in-love, Morgan, are campus pastors in West Palm Beach, FL.

To learn more about Pastor David, see what's on his mind, and be inspired by his leadership, follow along and connect on Facebook, Twitter, and Instagram.

# NOTES

_____

_____

_____

_____

_____

_____

_____

_____

_____

_____

_____

_____

# NOTES

_____

_____

_____

_____

_____

_____

_____

_____

_____

_____

_____

_____

_____

# NOTES

_____

_____

_____

_____

_____

_____

_____

_____

_____

_____

_____

_____

_____

# NOTES

_____

_____

_____

_____

_____

_____

_____

_____

_____

_____

_____

_____

_____

# NOTES

# NOTES

_____

_____

_____

_____

_____

_____

_____

_____

_____

_____

_____

_____

_____